WALT KAISER

CHAOS
to
HOPE
to
HEALING

Trusting Jesus in Turbulent Times

During my 15 years as a parish pastor, I was spared the experience Walt Waiser describes. The closest I've come to it was being unelected after nine years of difficult and challenging, but meaningful and fulfilling, service as president of a national church body. How I wish I had been able to read then what my longtime friend has now written. With skill, precision, sensitivity, candor, transparency, grace, and faithfulness, Walt takes the reader along on his emotional and spiritual journey of dealing with what he calls, "My Greatest Chaos." In the process, he shares how a painful experience has deepened his relationship with and trust in Jesus, Savior of the world and Lord of the universe.

Rev. Dr. Gerald B. Kieschnick
President Emeritus, The Lutheran Church—Missouri Synod
Chief Executive Officer, Legacy Deo

Few of us pray for the sort of pain and loss that brings real growth, but it comes nonetheless. Those who are willing to trust God completely during these wrenching seasons will find themselves led to a new place of peace, hope, love, joy, and freedom. Walt Waiser is one such pilgrim. Even as he discovers for himself the healing power of silence, solitude, prayer, and song, he is teaching us all where the Spirit of the Living God is to be found. Ultimately, Walt tells the eternal story of how, in our surrender, we come to Wisdom.

Heather Choate Davis
Writer, Speaker, Theologian

Walt invites us into his painful but redemptive journey with Jesus. The details of the journey may be uniquely Walt's, but the process he introduces is for each of us who have had our worlds turned upside-down. You can follow Walt because he is following Jesus.

Dr. Donald Christian
President and CEO, Concordia University Texas

With vulnerability and transparency, Walt Waiser shares how Jesus provided grace and guidance through turbulence and change. Chaos to Hope to Healing provides practical pathways and actions to meet personal chaos and see it transformed into hope.

Rev. Michael Newman
President-Elect, Texas District LCMS
Missions, Area C

Walt Waiser takes his readers with him on his personal journey to the desert and back, as he struggles to come to terms with a low blow that changes everything in his life. He points readers to specific tools the Lord provides to help us respond to the bad news headlines of everyday life in ways that keep us aligned with Jesus, caring for those around us, and growing new spiritual muscles.

John R Denninger
President, Southeastern District - LCMS

What does a person do when surprises or disappointments take the wind out of their sails...especially if you're a pastor? Walt Waiser experienced a major crisis in his ministry and life. This book shares what happened and how it affected his faith walk and his family. He invites the reader to join him on this journey of regaining joy, peace, and an excitement about the future. Practical advice is given from a seasoned wilderness traveler that can be helpful to others experiencing their own crisis.

Rev. Ken Hennings

One can respond to adversity, learn, and move forward in life—or react to adversity and move backwards in life and wallow in self-pity. This book is the story of how Walt responded to intense adversity in his life. We all are faced with adversity...how we deal with it is the key. We should learn from Walt on how God used him in different venues to grow the Kingdom. An excellent read.

Craig Faubel
Executive Coach

I'm delighted to recommend Walt's book to anyone who has been confronted with a traumatic change in life. As you read through it, you'll learn of the transformative power of God's grace and mercy—to change your heart from shock and anger to a new openness of joy and renewed mission. Join him in that journey, and the blessings of his transformation will bless you.

Pastor Jim Otte, LPC

Anger. Betrayal. Bitterness. Resentment. You won't find those between the covers of this book. What you will find is a heart-soothing meditation on clinging to Christ when a life crisis hits. If you walk with Christ long enough, you will endure moments where life doesn't make sense, answers are few, and friends seem in short supply. This book devotionally guides the reader towards a cross-centered approach to crisis—trusting that Jesus has an ultimate plan through His own suffering and betrayal on the cross. Walt shows us how to experience healing in the midst of your pain and forgiveness in your betrayals and also how to grow in a deeper relationship with Jesus in your darkest hours.

Rance Settle
Senior Pastor, Lamb of God Lutheran Church
Flower Mound, Texas

WALT WAISER

CHAOS
to
HOPE
to
HEALING

Trusting Jesus in Turbulent Times

TENTH
POWER

Elgin, IL · Tyler, TX

TENTHPOWERPUBLISHING

www.tenthpowerpublishing.com

Copyright © 2019 by Walt Waiser

All rights reserved. No part of this book may be reproduced without permission from the author, except by a reviewer quoting brief passages in a review; nor may any part of this book be reproduced, stored in a retrieval system or copied by mechanical photocopying, recording or other means without written permission from the author.

Scriptures taken from THE HOLY BIBLE, NEW INTERNATIONAL VERSION ®. Copyright© 1973, 1978, 1984, 2011 by Biblica, Inc.TM. Used by permission of Zondervan.

Scriptures marked RSV are taken from the REVISED STANDARD VERSION (RSV): Scripture taken from the REVISED STANDARD VERSION, Grand Rapids: Zondervan, 1971.

Scripture quotations taken from *THE MESSAGE*, copyright © 1993, 1994, 1995, 1996, 2000, 2001, 2002 by Eugene H. Peterson. Used by permission of NavPress. All rights reserved. Represented by Tyndale House Publishers, Inc.

Design by Inkwell Creative.

Softcover 978-1-938840-24-1
e-book 978-1-938840-19-7
10 9 8 7 6 5 4 3 2 1

To Vonnie, my bride. She is absolutely my partner in
life and ministry as we follow Jesus.

To our daughters, Heather and Amber, who grew up
at Peace, and their husbands Patrick and Peter.
Each of us felt the loss and continued to trust Jesus.

I wish to thank Craig Faubel, my corporate coach, who was the first to encourage me toward this book project,

I wish to thank Lynn Misch, without whom this manuscript would not have had a beginning. Lynn's coaching through the chapters helped this project get off to a great start.

I wish to thank Darlene Morrow and Sylvia Konrath. Their fine tuning in the editing process and encouragement was very significant.

I also wish to thank the people of Peace Lutheran, with whom I shared mission and ministry for over 38 years. I thank the people of Lamb of God Lutheran, with whom I have shared mission and ministry for the last four years.

TABLE OF CONTENTS

THE BEGINNING OF THE CHAOS

"May the God of hope fill you with all joy and peace as you trust in Him, so that you may overflow with hope by the power of the Holy Spirit." (Romans 15:13)

"The Board has voted unanimously..."

There is no easy way to share the news that I heard that night! Most often when someone asks, "What happened?" I respond, "You better sit down." The Mission and Ministry that had been my joy for over thirty-eight years in this Church Family now felt as if it were being ripped from my life. The Board had met without me, several times I suspect, and they had made a decision that would change everything.

It all came to an abrupt close when I was called to a Board of Directors meeting on Monday evening, January 27, 2014, at 6:30 p.m. The words of the message during that meeting were carefully chosen and repeated several times: "The Board has voted unanimously to go in a different direction in the position of senior pastor!"

The day before, on Sunday afternoon, I had received a text telling me to be sure to check my emails. I looked and found an email from the Board that stated I was to meet with them on Monday evening, and if other appointments were on my calendar, I was advised to reschedule them. Obviously, this was a very important meeting. Of all the subjects that might form the agenda for this meeting, the clear, specific message that they delivered that evening never entered my mind.

Indeed, I was shocked and stunned! It was one of those moments that causes you to shake your head and think, "This must be some horrible dream from which I need to wake up and come to my senses." The more I shook my head, the more I realized there would be no waking up! This was now "my new reality." The Board members were definite in their resolve that I needed to leave.

I struggled even to find the questions of clarification to ask. I finally got to the point of grasping the reality that they had "voted unanimously"—"Walt Waiser needs to leave!" All I could finally say was, "I will need some time to think and pray about this, and I will let you know my response to your decision." With that, I left the meeting and walked back to my office.

As I sat down to consider my next move, my most immediate concern was going home to my wife, Vonnie, to share "my new reality." I couldn't imagine a way to be clearly honest and yet guard her from the same stunning shock that I had experienced one hour earlier. I decided to call my son-in-law, who lives only five minutes from our home, to tell him the news I needed to share with Vonnie. I invited him to come over because he is a PhD psychologist, and I thought he might be able to help Vonnie hear this very difficult news. He came, but she did much better than I had dared to hope at hearing the news I had to deliver.

Much of the rest of that Monday night was a blur as we grappled to grasp this new reality that "the Board had voted unanimously to go in a different direction in the position of senior pastor." Vonnie's mind immediately went to the practical matters concerning finances and insurance. I remained basically shocked and stunned, and I began to ask, "God, what in the world does this mean?"

I went promptly to the Word of God and specifically to Romans 15:13 which formed my earliest prayer that night: "May the God of hope fill you with all joy and peace as you trust in Him, so that you may overflow with hope by the power of the Holy Spirit." That I could "overflow with hope" seemed an enormous stretch, but by "the power of the Holy Spirit," I prayed for the hope and joy and peace that I knew only He could provide in this context. Somehow, we got to sleep that night; I don't remember when.

Crux: A Puzzling or Difficult Problem

So here is the crux of the matter: Regardless of who we are, what we do, where we are in our faith journey following Jesus, whether we are young or older—how do we deal with adversity, loss, and pain? The reality for each of us, if we live and experience very much of life at all, is that we will all deal with adversity, loss, and pain! Where do we find the grace, strength, and courage to endure and to thrive?

As I begin to formulate the sharing of this story, it's November. For the last ten months of 2014, my primary connection to our God— Father, Son, and Spirit—has been through His Word. My times of solitude to meet with Him in His Word, and the prayer times I have had in response to His guiding me, have deepened my relationship with Him. He is the God of Hope, and He wants us to know in the depths of our souls that joy and peace that come only from Him.

In the midst of one such time of solitude, one of the most astounding things Jesus did in these ten months happened. It was on Friday, November 7, 2014. In my time of solitude that morning, He first led me to Job 1 and the listing of all the things that had been taken away from Job. That section closes with this summary: "At this, Job got up and tore his robe and shaved his head. Then he fell to the ground in worship...The LORD gave and the LORD has taken away; may the name of the LORD be praised" (Job 1:20–21). *Then* I was shocked again, and I had to ask, "Jesus, did You take this church away from me?" Quite honestly, I struggled even to let the words out of my mouth, but I did have to ask Him, "Jesus, did You take this church away from me?"

As disconcerting as the solitude was, it was a beautiful morning, so I took a very long walk near the water. As I walked, the Spirit led my thoughts back to Genesis 22, the chapter right after the birth of Isaac. There God said to Abraham, "Take your son, your only son, Isaac, whom you love, and go to the region of Moriah. Sacrifice him there as a burnt offering on one of the mountains I will tell you about" (Genesis 22:2).

In commanding Abraham to sacrifice his only son, Isaac, God is essentially challenging Abraham: Do you believe that I can take back this son you waited twenty-five years for and, now that you are well over one hundred years old, that I can still accomplish my promise to make a great nation of you?

In light of these reflections, I *had* to ask Jesus: "Did You take this church from me because You didn't know whether I would be willing to give her up as Abraham did? Are You challenging me to see whether I trust that You still have a plan and purpose for my life, even though You have taken from me this church that I have served for over thirty-eight years?"

The End of the Story?

This could easily become a story of injustice, anger, anxiety, bitterness, depression, and a strong desire to strike back! That is *not* what I want it to be, and that is *not* the way Jesus led me to respond, even from the first Tuesday morning, January 28. Beginning with that first morning, I have sought to find Jesus in the context of this adversity, loss, and pain. I have asked Him what He wants me to learn or discover about Him and His Sovereignty. I have repeatedly told Jesus, "I will follow *You* wherever *You* want me to go and do whatever *You* want me to do!"

I want to communicate the place to which Jesus has taken me, even before I share the process that He used to get me here. Please know that this process of Jesus taking me to this point is very significant. All the times of meditating on His Word and the prayers in response, all the hymns and songs of the church that He used to strengthen and encourage me with His promises, all the people who have prayed for Vonnie, me, and our family, and even the nine days of desert solitude in August—all these and more have been part of the process. I have been amazed by and so grateful for God's faithfulness in all of this.

I would only be lying were I to claim there has been no anger, anxiety, depression, or desire to strike back. A good friend affirmed, "Whenever you are ready to storm the castle, let me know, because I will be right beside you!" Even in the midst of the grief of letting go of a church I had served for over thirty-eight years, Jesus has led me to respond primarily by looking forward to the new adventure He has in mind for the next leg of the journey of following Him as His disciple. He amazes me regularly with the people with whom He puts me in contact and with the conversations I would never have imagined were coming.

I am still a bit uncertain as to specifically what led the Board to their decision, but it is obvious that I had lost their trust and confidence in me as their leader. It is true that several staff people had left, and they said it was because of me, but the Board had never had any conversation about their leaving with me. Nevertheless, whenever a leader, whatever the context, loses the trust and confidence of those he leads, then everything breaks down. On that Monday evening at that Board meeting, it became obvious to me that I had lost their trust and confidence, so they were going forward without me, and I would need to seek another direction of Jesus' leading.

Eugene Peterson in his book, *The Contemplative Pastor*, affirms, "The assumption of spirituality is that always God is doing something before I know it. So the task is not to get God to do something I think needs to be done, but to become aware of what God is doing so that I can respond to it and participate and take delight in it".[1] I first read those words in November of 1990, and they continue to be formative for my journey following Jesus. They echo what God said to His people in Jeremiah 29: "For I know the plans I have for you declares the LORD, plans to prosper you and not to harm you, plans to give you hope and a future. Then you will call upon me and come and pray to me, and I will listen to you. You will seek me and find me when you seek me with all your heart" (Jeremiah 29:11–13).

This is the other part of "my new reality"—God already knows the plans and purposes He has in place for me. I will do my best to "pray and seek Him with all my heart" and to pay attention to what I see Him doing around me, so that "I can respond and participate and take delight in it!" This has been a year of discovering where and when God is at work, discerning what He is already at work doing, and following His lead!

With that, I share this story of the gracious process Jesus used to lead me toward healing and guiding me in another direction.

Introduction: Questions for Reflection or Sharing

"May the God of hope fill you with all joy and peace as you trust in Him, so that you may overflow with hope by the power of the Holy Spirit."
(Romans 15:13)

Reflect on (and share) a time of difficult crisis in your life and how you discovered the hope you needed to persevere.

Was the difficulty the result of your decision or action, someone else's decision or action, or was it a medical diagnosis, and does it make any difference in finding hope?

Give a biblical example of someone who dealt with adversity, loss, or pain, and tell how that example has strengthened you.

What practices helped you find the grace and strength and courage to endure and thrive through this experience?

In your difficulties, what would it mean for you to say: "Jesus, I will follow You wherever You want me to go and do whatever You want me to do!"

What do you sense or discern God doing in your life now?

CHAPTER ONE

DISCOVERING GRACE AND STRENGTH AND COURAGE

"My grace is sufficient for you, for my power is made perfect in weakness." (2 Corinthians 12:9a)

The reality for each of us each day is that Jesus is always with us to provide the grace and strength and hope we need. The question is not: Is Jesus there and does He want to provide what we need? The question is: How do we access or tap into what we know Jesus wants to provide? Regardless of the adversity, loss, or pain with which we may wrestle, how do we reach out to the Jesus who is always present?

"...so that Christ's power may rest on me"

These are literally the powerful words of Jesus to Paul. They are powerful words about the power of Jesus available to Paul in the midst of dealing with whatever was his "thorn in the flesh." It is in response to these powerful words of Jesus that Paul made his absurd statement: "Therefore

I will boast all the more gladly about my weakness, so that Christ's power may rest on me" (2 Corinthians 12:9b). I have always loved these words of Jesus as He assures me, "My grace is sufficient." Jesus promises that His grace is all we need to deal with whatever difficulties we may encounter. I have always operated with the premise that the grace and power Jesus promised to Paul was not just his exclusively. That same grace and power is available to strengthen each of us in our difficulties.

While I love these words of promise from Jesus, Paul's response has always created a major conundrum for me. I crave Jesus' grace, which is always "sufficient for you." I resist the "I will boast all the more gladly about my weakness." I very much want "that Christ's power may rest on me," but is the only way for that to happen through boasting of my weakness? How could I honestly say what Paul did? I could honestly say, "I am ashamed of my weakness" or "I am humiliated by my weakness." How could I honestly say, "I will boast all the more gladly about my weakness?" How could I be anything but honest with this Jesus who knows each of my thoughts before I think them?

My major conundrum is that I want the promised grace and power of Jesus to "rest on me," and yet I resist Paul's encouragement to "boast of my weakness." Over at least the last twenty years, I have repeatedly said to Jesus, "I will continue to hold onto these words, because You have some real work to do to get me to Paul's response." I could not let go of these verses, because I needed to know more about Jesus' grace which is "sufficient for you," and "that Christ's power may rest on you."

So I have wrestled with these questions: How do we access the grace and power of Jesus in the midst of life's difficulties when we need them most? How do we gain entrance to this vast storehouse of strength, which only Jesus can provide? It is absolutely true that grace and strength and courage are available in abundance in relationship to Jesus. How does one take hold of them, claim them personally, and take them to heart in the midst of adversity, loss, and pain?

Dealing with Adversity, Loss, and Pain

As I began sharing this story, I already suggested that the crux of the matter, the issue I have been called to face more significantly than ever in this year of my life, is how do I deal with adversity, loss, and pain? When a person is younger, it may just be a matter of dealing with relatively smaller disappointments in life. However, sometimes major loss also happens earlier in life. At the age of twenty, my wife lost her much-loved father after his battle with cancer.

The reality is that each of us will have our own journey through adversity, loss, and pain. It's not whether or not we will have to deal with these difficulties. Each of us will have our own variations with which to deal. It is when we are called to face this journey that we have a choice to make. Will I face my pain in a healthy or an unhealthy manner? No one I know enjoys this journey, but each of us will make the choice, sometimes without any thought or intentionality, whether to do this in a healthy or in an unhealthy manner. I cannot define the journey in any specific way as if I am in control. I can decide to respond in ways that lead toward health or ways that leave me stuck dealing with the difficulty over and over again. We begin making this choice early in life, often in childish ways, and then we have an opportunity throughout life to learn to go in healthier directions. By the grace of God and the working of His Spirit, we can grow and choose to respond in a healthy way.

Dealing with difficulty is a complex situation that generally begins with children watching the adults around them and the ways the adults respond to the difficulties in their lives. Children will begin by imitating what they see. If they see the significant others around them responding to pain by denying a problem exists, or by avoiding the issue with other distractions, or putting the blame on others for what they need to deal with, or by participating in an ongoing pity party, then children may get stuck in a cycle of anger, sadness, anxiety, and fear. If children see the significant others around them responding to pain by facing it with the grace and strength that only Jesus can supply and walking through the darkness following Jesus, then children can learn to respond to their pain with courage and resilience.

Typically, each of us begins by dealing poorly with our difficulties. It is just like learning anything; we need to have a chance to practice, practice, and practice. Life in this sinful world seems to give each of us ample opportunities to practice. Hopefully, by the grace of God and the opportunities life provides, we can grow toward responding with grace and strength and courage.

"Consider It Pure Joy When You Face Trials"

James also presents me with another scriptural conundrum with which I have wrestled for many years. He begins his letter with this strange encouragement: "Consider it pure joy, my brothers, whenever you face trials of many kinds" (James 1:2). When I first discovered this verse, I wanted to say to James, "You must be kidding me! No one I know finds joy, pure or otherwise, in the trials they have to face!" Therefore, I have another conundrum. Paul encourages me to find grace and power in weakness. James encourages me to find "pure joy in facing trials of many kinds." So I begin to ask, "Am I to learn that Jesus encourages me to find His grace in those life experiences that seem to deny it? Am I to learn that Jesus leads me to find *Him* in those life experiences that seem to deny Him and His power and presence?"

I have been learning precisely that in this journey of following Jesus. Especially in this year of dealing with such significant adversity, loss, and pain, I am learning to seek Jesus as never before. I am learning to seek Jesus and not to seek grace, strength, courage, joy, and hope. While my relationship with Jesus is deepening, I am discovering that I have all the grace, strength, courage, joy, and hope that I need. All that I need flows naturally from a deepening relationship with Jesus. It may seem a subtle shift in thinking, but it is Jesus that I need. As I continue to grow in relationship with Jesus, then the One who knows me better than I know myself will supply exactly what I need, exactly when I need it.

This is the reason that James goes on to amplify his strange encouragement by saying, "Because you know that the testing of your faith develops perseverance. Perseverance must finish its work so that you may be mature and complete, not lacking anything. If any of you lacks wisdom, he should ask God, who gives generously to all without finding fault, and it will be given to him" (James 1:3–5). Now, this side of heaven, not one of us will reach absolute maturity and completeness. Nevertheless, each day of our earthly journey of faith can be one of letting Jesus grow us through perseverance toward maturity and completeness. As I let Him deepen the relationship we have, He will produce joy in me even in the midst of "trials of many kinds."

I love James' encouragement toward wisdom. If we don't know what to do, as is often the case in the midst of trials and difficulties, just ask God! Our God of grace loves to give wisdom in great abundance to those who just ask Him! If we need wisdom to discern the way, just ask God! Eugene Peterson in *The Message* shares some unique insights into James in the Introduction to this letter: "According to church traditions, James carried the nickname 'Old Camel Knees' because of thick calluses built up on his knees from many years of determined prayer. The prayer is foundational to the wisdom. Prayer is always foundational to wisdom."[2] The times of daily prayer, whether kneeling, standing, or sitting will give God the opportunity to provide the wisdom necessary to persevere.

I Have Never Been So Carried by Jesus!

I am not seeking grace, or strength, or courage, or joy, or anything. I am seeking Jesus! I am keeping the eyes of my faith focused on Jesus! I want a deepening relationship with Jesus, who promises to provide whatever I need, regardless of the trials I encounter in this faith journey following Him. I began saying to numerous people in the spring of the year of "my new reality," "I don't think I have ever been so carried by Jesus!" I have never before thought that thought, so I have never before said those words. I found myself saying to people who expressed their concern for me, "I don't think I have ever been so carried by Jesus!"

To me, women seem to have a visual image of Jesus carrying them in His arms. That is most often the way a man will carry a woman. He will pick her up and carry her in his arms. That is not the way a man carries another man. When a man carries another man, he carries him on his back. That is my visual image of Jesus carrying me; He is carrying me on His back. So I would regularly say, "I don't think I have ever been so carried by Jesus, and it is a very good place to be!"

I found myself saying that I will "depend on Jesus" to provide whatever I need for this task or meeting or sermon. I found myself speaking more regularly of my "reliance on Jesus"— depending on, and relying on, and being carried by Jesus, so that He provided whatever I needed to take me each step of this year. It's a whole new depth of relationship with Jesus. So I find that my words are different than Paul's; I am not exactly "boasting of my weakness." Yet I believe I am acknowledging my dependence and my reliance on Jesus, and also my weakness, so that "Christ's power may rest on me." I am using slightly different words, yet I am seeking the very same results—so that "Christ's power may rest on me."

Two Disciplines and Three Resources

Without a doubt, a relationship to Jesus is the only way to persevere and mature and find joy and wisdom. It's *all* about Jesus! It's *only* about Jesus! It's *always* about Jesus! So let's go back to the previous questions: How do we access the grace and power of Jesus in the midst of life's difficulties when we need them most? How do we gain entrance to this vast storehouse of strength that only Jesus can provide?

For me, in the midst of dealing with the most significant adversity, loss, and pain of my life, I found myself going back to the most significant places in which I had been with Jesus and had drawn strength from Him in the past. The two devotional disciplines that became most significant for me were journaling and creating times of solitude. Writing down my reflections, thoughts, meditations, and prayers became a much greater necessity. While earlier in my life I struggled to develop a meaningful pattern of being alone with God in solitude, in this year, being alone with God took on a deeper meaning.

The substance of so much of my journaling in the midst of these recent times of solitude has gone back to three primary resources of faith. Each took on a renewed importance for being with Jesus and drawing on His grace and strength and courage. First, was the Word of God, especially meditating on Jesus as the Word. Second, were times of prayer in response to meditating on the Word. Third, were the hymns and songs of the faithful. These two disciplines and three resources have been my most important ways of being with Jesus and drawing from Him what I have needed. These have deepened my relationship with God—Father, Son, Spirit.

First, I will share more about the two disciplines and how each became so significant for me in following Jesus more faithfully. Second, I will share how the three resources became woven into the fabric of the events and months of this year of my life. Each of the three—the Word, prayer, and singing the songs of the faith—had powerfully shaped my faith and life prior to this year. In this year, they have more powerfully shaped and deepened my relationship with the Jesus I seek to follow.

Chapter One: Questions for Reflection or Sharing

"My grace is sufficient for my power is made perfect in weakness."
(2 Corinthians 12:9)

Do you know anyone like Paul who has been so transparent with his/her weakness?

What are some examples of unhealthy ways you see people around you dealing with their loss and pain?

What are some examples of healthy ways you see people around you responding to their loss and pain?

What are some helpful practices you have discovered to let Jesus deepen His relationship with you?

Have you experienced a time when Jesus carried you? Do you want Jesus to carry you through your times of loss or pain? How do you find Joy in Jesus when facing trials?

JOURNALING AS THE WAY TO STAY ALERT, ATTENTIVE, AND RECEPTIVE TO JESUS' LEADING

"Thus may the power of my Lord Christ be strong within me and His peace invade my spirit."

—John Baillie, A Diary of Private Prayer

"And surely I am with you always," these are the powerful words of promise Jesus speaks to us all. Since Jesus spoke this promise some 2,000 years ago, many of His followers have relied on this promise to bring strength, trust, and hope in the midst of great difficulty. While the words of promise are there for all, many struggle with fear, panic, and distress. A regularly-practiced relationship with Jesus can be the key that unlocks the door to discover His waiting presence.

JANUARY 28, 2014 at 5:40 a.m.

This is part of my journal entry for Tuesday, the day after the Board told me of their decision:

> "As of last night, after thirty-eight years, my future and the future of this Church Family are no longer tied together. They are headed off 'in another direction.' The Board of Directors informed me of their decision last night. I will not seek to blame or accuse anyone else—everyone else. I will not be angry. I probably will be angry along the way, but I will seek to deal with the anger in healthy ways so that I do not end up responding to everyone in anger.
>
> I need to be true to myself in this!
>
> I need to consider what the best is for this Church Family!
>
> I need *You* to give me the wisdom and insight to understand how I need to move forward!
>
> Jesus, Help Me! 'Thus let the power of my Lord Christ be strong within me and His peace invade my spirit.' Jesus, Help Me!"

According to Webster's Dictionary, a journal is "a record of experiences, ideas, or reflections kept regularly for private use."[3] For some, journaling may seem a very non-essential use of time. For others of us, journaling is absolutely an integral, intentional, essential use of time. In my morning solitude, my journal comes out early. Generally, I begin with the singing of a hymn or song of the faith, and then I go to my journal. It enables me to focus my thoughts on the God with whom

I need this time of solitude. My journal is most easily described as a running conversation I have with God. It is a bit like thinking aloud in His presence and staying sensitive to the places He may take my thoughts.

On the first morning after discovering "my new reality," I went early to my journal. As I recorded the thoughts that came, I was led to part of a prayer from John Baillie's *A Diary of Private Prayer.* This will not surprise those who know me, because I have been praying as John leads since April of 1980. Any devotional resource like Baillie's where I find deep and meaningful in my walk with Jesus, whenever I have the opportunity, I share and encourage others to make use of that same resource.

That morning January 28, I was taken to the close of John's prayer for the evening of the thirteenth day. I have lived with and prayed these prayers for so many years that the Spirit of Jesus will often bring to mind the specific prayer I need exactly when I need it. I still remember the very evening that the last line of this prayer first became so significant for me. It was at least fifteen years ago, and I'd had one of "those meetings." There were only five of us present, but all the wheels fell off halfway through the meeting. It was very disconcerting and left everyone feeling very unsettled.

I don't know what the others who were present did, but when I went home, I could not go to sleep. After lying in bed for a while, I got up and went to my study. I returned to my good friend, John Baillie, and, yes, it was the thirteenth evening of the month. This evening prayer begins in a powerful way: "O Heavenly Father, give me a heart like the heart of Jesus Christ. . . ".[4] And the last line of this prayer really stuck: "Thus let the power of my Lord Christ be strong within me and His peace invade my spirit".[5] To begin by praying, "give me a heart like the heart of Jesus" and then to pray, "and His peace invade my spirit" is a powerful prayer. Baillie was an incredible wordsmith, and praying for the peace of Jesus to "invade my spirit" enables peace to begin small in my heart and expand until it fills me. I believe that because it was the last conscious thought I prayed that night, it was the first conscious thought I prayed the next morning.

Why Journaling?

Over the years, as I have sought to follow Jesus, journaling is the way He has shaped my daily devotional time of solitude with Him. To put my thoughts and prayers in writing keeps me more focused on Jesus. To go early to my journal helps clear assorted cluttered thoughts and points me clearly toward Jesus. The more clearly the focus stays on Jesus, the more He can shape the time we spend together. He does all the important work in me and on me. My primary cooperative responsibility is to show up, and open up, to let Him do whatever He chooses.

Yet, I must confess that when I began journaling, it did feel a bit silly to me. I kept wondering why I couldn't just think and pray? Why did I need to write things down? Then came a devotional resource from *The Upper Room* in Nashville entitled *Alive Now*. In one particular monthly issue, they wanted to encourage journaling, so they did something very unique. On the left page, they put a Scripture passage that they wanted the reader to reflect and meditate on; on the right page, they put nothing at all. The blank right page was an encouragement to write or journal any reflections, meditations, thoughts, or feelings—whatever God may be causing to happen in one's mind and heart—in response to the Scriptures.

The only experience I had ever had with journaling before this was on two prior trips to Israel. I had wanted to hold onto absolutely every single thing that I saw, heard, felt, smelled, sensed, tasted, and touched. During these trips, I had been quite disciplined to begin and end each day by journaling everything I could think of. Throughout the day, I would journal anything that I sensed was significant. Those journaling experiences had a very clear and specific focus, and they enabled me to hold onto and remember much more of the details of those incredible trips.

This journaling experience seemed much more random, and frankly, non-essential than had my prior journaling experiences. Nevertheless, at the encouragement of that issue of *Alive Now*, I began to wade out into the waters of journaling. I wrote down the reflections, thoughts, and feelings that came to my mind and heart as I meditated on each of the Scripture passages. There were only fifteen or so exercises on which to journal. By the time I got to the end of that month's issue, I found myself intrigued! I was beginning to realize that something about writing my thoughts and prayers down led me to be much more attentive and receptive to God's guiding. *That* is the key to deep and meaningful solitude time with our God—Father, Son, Spirit—being attentive and receptive to His work in us and on us, through His Word. We do *none* of the important work in the solitude. Our cooperative responsibility is simply to show up, and open up, and let the Spirit of our Lord do all the important work to shape us as disciples of Jesus. Our lifetime journey of faith is an ongoing process of regularly showing up, and opening up, to let the Spirit of Jesus shape and mold us to become more like Him. Obviously, this side of heaven we will never become just like Jesus! The still ongoing process is what Jesus will continue in each of us.

Jesus told His twelve disciples to follow Him. They were to follow and watch everything that He did, and said, and taught. As a rabbi, Jesus wanted to show His disciples all He could, teach them everything He knew, so that they could become like Him. Jesus did all He could for three years to invest Himself in these twelve, so that they could become like Him, so that they could imitate Him. The most significant way that we follow Jesus today, the most significant time we spend with Jesus, is as we meet Him in His written Word. Jesus still invests Himself in us through His Word, so that we 21st century disciples might imitate Him.

Intentionally Being Attentive

As I mentioned before, on my first two trips to Israel, I wanted to hold onto absolutely as much of everything as I could. Others who have made this trip to the land of Jesus also know this urgency. Anyone who has waited, and planned, and eagerly anticipated any trip to a distant place that is very important to him or her can sense this urgency. It just becomes important to hold onto and remember every sight, sound, and memory. I have done the same thing on mission trips to Honduras and India. It is so amazing to see all that God is at work doing in the lives of people, and I have each time wanted to remember each sight, and sound, and story. The discipline of journaling has kept me more attentive to God and has helped me hold onto, remember, and treasure each sight of God's activity.

It began to seem natural to bring home what I have so valued in distant and foreign lands. I wanted to stay alert to, be attentive to, and live receptive to whatever God might be doing on these trips, and I needed to have these same disciplines in the midst of my daily journey of faith. My daily life is much less exciting than one of my trips, but there is a growing sense that I want to be just as intentional in noticing all that Jesus is doing in my everyday life as I am on my travels. As I follow Jesus each day, I want to stay alert to, be attentive to, and live receptive to whatever Jesus wants to do each day in me and through me.

The truth I realized is that as surely as Jesus called the twelve to follow Him, He also called me to follow Him. As surely as He wanted to shape and mold the twelve to become like Him, He wants to shape and mold me to become like Him. Jesus does all the most important work. My cooperative responsibility is to show up, and open up, and let His Spirit form me to become more like Jesus.

I will never achieve complete Christ-likeness; no one ever will. Nevertheless, it is what Paul encourages the Ephesians toward as he says, "Until we all reach unity in the faith and in the knowledge of the Son of God and become mature, attaining to the whole measure of the fullness of Christ" (Ephesians 4:13). The important part is not seeking to measure the completeness, but continuing in the process. Since every human lives every day in his sinful nature, no one will ever "attain the whole measure of the fullness of Christ." Movement forward in this process that is led by the Spirit of Jesus through the written Word is precisely what God intends for each of us who follows Jesus.

So I began to consider that Jesus has called me to follow Him, and that means each step of every day. I wish I could say that I do follow Him each step of every day, but I cannot. I can say that that is the direction toward which I want to grow. If that is the direction toward which I want Jesus to grow me, it will require some intentionality. The Spirit of Jesus is the only one who can grow me as a disciple, but that generally requires some active cooperation from me. The Word of God and the Sacraments Jesus gave are the powerful means the Spirit uses to grow us. If I do not actively show up to receive these means, if they are available, but I do not take advantage of them, my growth will be hindered.

With this in mind, I began to wonder to myself what might increase my intentionality to show up in the ways the Spirit uses to grow me as a disciple. What might help me stay alert to, be attentive to, and live receptive to the things Jesus may be actively doing around me? Since journaling had been so helpful on my trips, might it serve the same purpose in my daily life? I wish I could say that I journal every day, and that I watch for every way that Jesus is active around me. Nevertheless, the truth is that journaling does help me stay alert to, attentive to, and receptive to Jesus' working in my life.

The Practice of Journaling

The morning of January 28, 2014, is when I particularly needed to be alert to, attentive to, and receptive to Jesus. I needed Jesus to show up to calm and quiet my spirit and to lead me to discern how He wanted me to move forward. It was easier to figure out some of the ways I could respond and some of the ways I wanted to respond. In that first early morning of "my new reality," I am thankful that Jesus led me to wonder what He wanted me to do. He led me to journal, "Jesus, Help Me! 'Thus let the power of my Lord Christ be strong within me and His peace invade my spirit.' Jesus, Help Me!" I did not discern His plan or direction for me to move forward that morning, or for several more weeks. On that first morning, it was helpful to begin asking Him what He wanted me to do and to begin to acknowledge my reliance and dependence on Him.

I first thought the words of that Baillie prayer: "Thus may the power of my Lord Christ be strong within and His peace invade my spirit." Then, I journaled the words of that prayer. Then I prayed aloud the words of that prayer. On mornings like this one, it is often difficult to take hold of the promises of Jesus. It is difficult to claim them personally and take them to heart. I find that writing the words, often writing them again and again, helps me to take hold of the Jesus who promises, "My grace is sufficient." Writing these words again and again enabled "His peace to invade my spirit." I have always been grateful to Baillie that he chose the word "invade" to pray for Jesus' peace. It was precisely an invasion of Jesus' peace that I needed. I needed His "peace that passes all understanding" to invade my spirit.

There is nothing magical about journaling that changes everything and makes it all better. Yet, somehow getting the thoughts out of my head and on paper makes them clearer, more specific, and easier to consider. Journaling does keep me more alert to, attentive to, and receptive to what Jesus is doing and what He wants me to do. Discerning Jesus' plans and purposes is always the goal, since His direction is always better than mine is. Journaling enables me to be more intentionally attentive to Jesus.

Chapter Two: Questions for Reflection or Sharing

Jesus, Help Me! "Thus let the power of my Lord Christ be strong within me, and His peace invade my spirit." Jesus, Help Me! [6]

Have you ever experimented with journaling, or has another discipline helped you stay alert to and attentive to Jesus as you seek to follow Him?

What activities have you discovered to be helpful the morning after you learn of a crisis in your life?

How do you stay receptive to the leading of Jesus in order to discern His direction for your life?

What are some significant means that Jesus uses to continue the process to shape and mold you to become more like Him?

What are some of the indicators that Jesus is at work to mature you as you follow Him?

When and how do you "show up and open up" for Jesus to continue His work in your life?

CHAPTER THREE

STRENGTHENED THROUGH SOLITUDE WITH JESUS

"Yet the news about him spread all the more, so that crowds of people came to hear him and to be healed of their sicknesses. But Jesus often withdrew to lonely places and prayed." (Luke 5:15–16)

Solitude can be both one of the most frightening and one of the most calming experiences of human existence. Solitude with His Father was definitely the pattern of Jesus' life and mission. Even for followers of Jesus, few have a practiced pattern of solitude so that Jesus can restore their souls. In this hyper-connected culture in which we live, it requires intentionality to unplug and seek a place of quiet with Jesus; and for those who do so, He restores their souls.

The Definite Pattern of Jesus' Life and Ministry

Solitude for prayer was obviously the pattern of Jesus' life. Other gospel verses will say, "Very early in the morning, while it was still dark, Jesus got up, left the house and went off to a solitary place, where he prayed" (Mark 1:35). Another gospel verse says, "One of those days Jesus went out to a mountainside to pray, and spent the night praying to God" (Luke 6:12). While the powerful narrative of the Transfiguration may overshadow the story, it begins with Jesus in prayer: "About eight days after Jesus said this, he took Peter, John and James with him and went up onto a mountain to pray. As he was praying, the appearance of his face changed, and his clothes became as bright as a flash of lightning" (Luke 9:28–29). A fuller listing of these verses continues to evidence that solitude for prayer was the pattern of Jesus' life.

In Matthew 14, two very distinct and different events cause the same response of solitude for prayer in Jesus. One is a major tragedy, and the other a major triumph. At the beginning of Chapter 14, John the Baptist is beheaded at the whim of Herod's vindictive wife. The record of this event closes by saying, "John's disciples came and took his body and buried it. Then they went and told Jesus. When Jesus heard what had happened, he withdrew by boat privately to a solitary place" (Matthew 14:12–13). When Jesus heard of this horrible tragedy suffered by his cousin, He needed to go off and spend time alone with the Father.

What follows in the same chapter is the well-known, "Feeding of the 5,000," which obviously was the feeding of the 7,000 or 9,000, when all the women and children who accompanied those 5,000 men were included. Here is the summary that closes this incredible event: "Immediately Jesus made the disciples get into the boat and go on ahead of him to the other side, while he dismissed the crowd. After he had dismissed them, he went up on a mountainside by himself to pray" (Matthew 14:22–23). After this demonstration of His power as the Son of God that was witnessed by thousands of people, Jesus needed to go off and spend time alone with the Father.

The gospels make it clear that even in the midst of having only three years to complete the mission the Father sent Him to accomplish, Jesus knew that solitude was virtually imperative. Before and after major events, Jesus made it a priority to take time to go off to be alone with the Father. While it makes a strong impression to see the whole list of verses noting the times Jesus went off for solitude, the Luke 5 passage noted above establishes the pattern of His life and mission. There could not have been a greater urgency because of the crowds of people pressing forward to be with Jesus, "but Jesus often withdrew to lonely places and prayed." Jesus had only three years to help the twelve grasp the reality that He was the Son of God. He had only a short time to explain exactly what it would mean for Him to become the Savior of the world through His death and resurrection. He had only this brief period to train them as His disciples for the mission they would take over after His ascension to continue to spread the Good News of God's grace. "*But* yet He often withdrew to lonely places and prayed," and that sends a powerful message for us as His disciples!

Others Who Call Us to Solitude

In the spirit of this pattern of Jesus, Henri Nouwen in his book, *Making All Things New*, asserts this: "Without solitude it is virtually impossible to live a spiritual life. Solitude begins with a time and a place for God and him alone. If we really believe not only that God exists but also that he is actively present in our lives—healing, teaching and guiding—we need to set aside a time and space to give him our undivided attention". [7]

Wow! While Nouwen's assertion seems absolutely consistent with the life and practice of Jesus, when I read it for the first time, it was about as far away from my life and practice as the other side of the world. Even then I would have affirmed that I wanted God to be "actively present in my life—healing, teaching, and guiding," but going off alone in solitude with Him was *not* the pattern of my life. Not only was it not my pattern, but also when I first read these words that Nouwen may have meant for encouragement, I experienced them more like a cold, hard slap in the face. Not only was solitude not the pattern of my life, but it was also a rather frightening thought.

Solitude was a frightening concept to me, because when it comes to the continuum of extrovert at one end and introvert at the other, I almost fall off the extrovert end. I have always loved being with and around people. That is what has always energized me! Even as a boy of only ten or twelve years old, if I had been asked to lead a group in prayer, I would have been glad to do so. That is part of what led me to be so eager to pursue pastoral ministry, because I loved being with and serving others in Jesus' name.

While many of the aspects of the office of public ministry came more naturally for me, this pattern of solitude that Jesus practiced and that Nouwen was calling me toward was as foreign to me as the Chinese language. Early in my ministry as I read more and more about Jesus and solitude, I could see it was His pattern, but I didn't have the slightest clue about how to begin to copy this pattern. Introverts love this "time and place for God and him alone," but extroverts fear it. That is not an overstatement, because I was afraid to go off alone to be with God. I felt a need to seek solitude, but I was afraid. Part of me wanted to go off to be alone with God, but part of me resisted.

I suspect that most people think that this solitude with God stuff comes naturally for clergy. Don't all pastors just love spending time alone with God? I began asking around in my early years of ministry, and if those pastors who "loved spending time alone with God" were around, either I couldn't find them or they would not talk to me about their times of solitude.

Then, in 1986, I discovered a wonderful resource by John Doberstein entitled, *Minister's Prayer Book*. What he said in the Introduction both encouraged and frightened me. Here is what he shared: "There can be no question of the centrality of prayer and reading in the minister's life. And yet, the constant confession we hear when ministers grow candid is that increasingly they have no time for prayer and study... Where will the minister, caught in a net of multitudinous responsibilities, find the quietness which will give him strength and give power and authority to his preaching and pastoral work? When will he concentrate upon prayer for the Holy Spirit, who it is true, bids us be sensitive to the voices of the world, but also liberates us from bondage to them?". [8] I was that pastor "caught in a net of multitudinous responsibilities" who could not find time to pray. At least I didn't value solitude enough to go seek it, or perhaps it was easier just to avoid the whole subject. The *problem* was that the more I avoided solitude, the emptier I became. Finally, the emptiness got too large to avoid or deny any longer, and I had to go seeking.

A Time to Walk the Walk

By this time I had read plenty of resources, both biblical and others, to convince me of the need for solitary time alone with God. The only thing standing in the way was my fear of being alone or, more precisely, my fear of being alone with God! How crazy was that? I had been born to parents who brought me for baptism when I was less than one month old, where I was marked with the cross of Jesus on my forehead and on my heart. I had grown up attending worship and Sunday school throughout my childhood. I had grown to know God's grace in the cross of Jesus through my confirmation. My faith journey had continued throughout high school. In spite of ups and downs, and slips and falls along the way, I never had a moment when I didn't believe Jesus' words that He would be "with me always."

It was time to walk the walk, to explore stillness, and quiet, and solitude alone with God. I decided that instead of going to the office for a regular day of work, I would follow Jesus into a day of solitude. I went that morning to a nearby lake, because water is always so renewing to my spirit. I took my devotional resources—journal, John Baillie, Bible for meditation—and I went off to explore and seek a meaningful day of solitude alone with God. To be honest, it was disconcerting and got me way out of my comfort zone. I did it, nevertheless, because the need had become too great for the "healing, teaching and guiding" to fill some of the emptiness that was consuming my spirit. So I went off to explore solitude, to discover meaningful time with our God—Father, Son, Spirit. I prayed for the Spirit to guide my time as I journaled and meditated on Scripture, and prayed, and walked near the water.

By the grace of God, the good news is that as I faced the fear with Jesus present, He began to fill the emptiness. It didn't happen all at once, but it was the beginning of the process. I didn't hear any voices speak from the clouds. I discovered no special revelation from the Spirit. I didn't see Jesus appear in any unique or unusual way. I began to ponder and meditate on some verses that most often get overlooked in one of the best-known of all the psalms. In Psalm 23 it seems to me that we generally go from, "The LORD is my shepherd, I shall not be in want" (verse 1), and then skip down to, "Even though I walk through the valley of the shadow of death, I will fear no evil" (verse 4). As powerful as those verses are, we often overlook, "He makes me lie down in green pastures, he leads me beside quiet waters, he restores my soul" (verses 2–3).

In some of those early eight-hour days of solitude, I began to focus on and consider these often overlooked words of Psalm 23. The more I meditated on these verses, the more it occurred to me that if I do not make the time to slow the pace and quiet the noise in my life, then I will generally not let the Shepherd make me lie down in green pastures and lead me beside quiet waters so that He restores my soul. More and more,

I began to love that visual picture of Jesus taking me to a beautiful green meadow to make me lie down beside a quiet stream. Lying down in the soft, green grass and listening to the quiet sounds of that gently flowing water, Jesus restores my soul.

Now Jesus could literally *make* me lie down in green pastures, but that is not His intention. I have come to understand these words more as His invitation to join Him in solitude. It is as if Jesus wants us to hear Him inviting us to come to this quiet place and let Him do those things in us that will restore, and renew, and refresh our souls. That was exactly what I began to experience as I followed Him into the solitude. I began the practice each month to take one day to go off to that picnic table near the lake with my devotional resources to explore meaningful times of solitude with God—Father, Son, and Spirit. It was just like anything else that I didn't know how to do. I just needed to begin somewhere and then practice, practice, practice. The more time I spent regularly in solitude with God, the more meaningful it became.

I don't recall exactly how many of those eight-hour days I went to the lake, but along the way I began to wonder what it might be like to explore a twenty-four hour period of solitude. So I went off to one of our nearby State Parks and slept in my van. (During the week, especially during the school year, our State Parks in Texas offer wonderful places of quiet.) I took the same devotional resources, but this time I had a fire and a lantern in the evening, so I could continue to read, and journal, and pray. I don't know just how many of the twenty-four hour retreats I did before I began to wonder about doing a forty-eight hour retreat. That led me to develop a pattern of a forty-eight hour retreat once each quarter. It was not a time to work, but a time to be alone with God for solitude so that He might restore my soul. I journaled and meditated on Scripture, and I prayed and read material that encouraged me to be intentional about my own spiritual journey.

A Calling to the Desert for Solitude

By now my devotional pattern had grown into seeking five one-hour periods of morning solitude, because I am a morning guy. Then, once a quarter, I went off for forty-eight hours of solitude with Jesus, away from the office and work. I discovered that this was the pattern that kept me spiritually refreshed and attentive to what Jesus might be doing around me. I would love to say that five one-hour mornings was exactly what I did every week, but I would just be blowing smoke. Even when I got off-track with the weekly discipline, the forty-eight hour retreats were generally the corrective action I needed to get back on track. I discovered that five one-hour mornings and a forty-eight hour retreat each quarter was the devotional pattern that kept me spiritually refreshed and most attentive to the activity of Jesus in my life.

As I continued to meditate on Scripture, there just seemed to be something unique about the desert or the wilderness. In Exodus 3, Moses was keeping the flocks of his father-in-law, Jethro, in the Sinai desert when he encountered God in the burning bush. After the children of Israel left Egypt, they formed their covenant relationship with God in the desert at the foot of Mt. Sinai. I have seen the lonely hillsides outside Bethlehem where David kept his father's sheep and where God no doubt planted many of the psalms in his mind and heart. Those hillsides look more like wilderness than lush, green farmland. Many may be surprised to learn that Paul, right after his Damascus road experience with Jesus, went off into the Arabian Desert before he began his missionary journeys. The "After many days had gone by" (Acts 9:23) is further defined by Galatians 1:15–17. There Paul clearly says, "But when God who set me apart from birth and called me by his grace, was pleased to reveal his Son in me so that I might preach him among the Gentiles, I did not consult any man, nor did I go up to Jerusalem to see those who were apostles before I was, but I went immediately into Arabia and later returned to Damascus" (Galatians 1:15–17). Paul spent time in the Arabian Desert before beginning his mission.

By this time in my life, I had been to Israel twice and had seen some of the desolate places to which Jesus might well have gone off alone. I was beginning to be fascinated about what goes on in the desert. It was alluring and yet frightening. To go off alone with God for forty-eight hours in a State Park, even in the middle of the week when no one else was around, that was one thing. To do what Paul did, in a place far more remote, seemed entirely different.

The closest desert I knew was Big Bend National Park in far southwestern Texas. It seems so remote because it is on the way to absolutely nothing! You really have to *want* to go to this wilderness! I have lived in this state my whole life, with only a few years of exile for schooling, but I had never been to Big Bend. I had seen pictures that looked similar to places I had seen in Israel, so I thought that this might be the place I needed to go. Even with a good number of solitary retreats under my belt, this one was a much bigger step into the unknown.

It was time once again to get out of my comfort zone and make this Elijah-like journey to the desert of Big Bend. I proposed to the Board of Elders that I would take a one-month Sabbatical in January of 1990, the first week of which I would spend in the desert of Big Bend. Unfortunately, they agreed with my proposal, so I had no way out. I still remember heading southwest out of Fort Worth thinking that this had to be the stupidest thing I had ever thought of doing! About two hours out of town, I so wanted to turn around and go back home. If I had not already told so many people what I was doing, I think I would have turned around and said, "Forget about it!" Oftentimes, accountability is a good thing.

An Alluring Location That Is Satisfying to the Soul

I arrived at the Visitor Center in Big Bend and settled on the "remote site" called Kbar. In one sense, it was a beautiful site, because I could look to the east and watch the sun rise over the Sierra Del Carmen Mountains and look to the west to see the sun set behind the Chisos Mountains in the middle of the park. In another sense, the words "remote site" were to be taken seriously. I drove two-and-one-half miles straight into the desert off the main road and stayed for one week in my van. The desert was both fascinating and frightening! I didn't see another human being for those seven days, until I left. The only other sign of life I saw was a bird that flew by on the third day, going God only knows where. At the end of the second day, I realized that other than the wind, I had not heard a sound that I didn't make. Several times, I just had to yell aloud for a bit.

On the cloudy nights, there was no other source of light except mine—no headlights, no streetlights, nothing overhead, a complete absence of ambient light of any kind. I was there just after a new moon, so there was no moon even on the clear nights, just the deepest, darkest night sky with billions and billions of stars in the Milky Way Galaxy! At first I was painfully aware that only God and I were out there, but then that reality became good news!

That first evening in the desert, when the sun (even behind the clouds) sets before six in early January was when I experienced the most fear. The Park authorities had taken away my fire—something about a drought—although only God knows how the sand and rocks of the desert could burn. Therefore, I could use none of the firewood that I had brought, and a fire somehow meant both warmth and protection. Without a fire, when the sun set in January in the desert, it was *cold*! It was too early to go to sleep, and I couldn't light my lantern inside the van without the windows open for ventilation (colder still), so I read for a while with my handy dandy flashlight. I discovered that reading by flashlight was quite an interesting task. After a while, it seemed like my eyes were beginning to cross and my vision began to get a bit fuzzy. As uncomfortable as I was, it was still too early to try to go to sleep. Taking a walk didn't seem like much of an alternative. I didn't have a cell phone in those days; I still don't know whether one can make a call from that remote site even today. I crawled into my sleeping bag just to stay warm, and I mean all the way into the bag! I *first* began to think of the nasty guys who come across the Rio Grande River and do whatever they want to do to defenseless campers they find. A country boy from Texas always has a pocketknife, but that was mainly for peeling oranges, not for defending myself. *Then* I began to wonder if something did happen to me out there in the middle of nowhere—snake bite, broken arm, or deep cut from my sharp pocketknife—how long would it be before someone came looking for me? Then I thought to myself that I could either be afraid that someone was going to find me, or I could be afraid that no one would ever find me... *but* I couldn't be afraid of both of those things at the same time. That makes no sense, but fear is often irrational.

I pulled my flashlight out again and went back to all the most significant Scripture passages that had always given me a sense of God's presence and power. I could not find one that night that would cut the fear. Then I went back to all the sections of John Baillie's prayers that had always been so meaningful and comforting, but nothing cut the fear. Then I pulled out my hymnal—*Lutheran Worship* in those days— and began to *sing* the hymns of the Church. I didn't just read them or think about them; I sang them aloud! I turned to the section of evening hymns and the first one was:

All praise to thee, my God, this night for all the blessings of the light.

Keep me, oh, keep me, King of kings, beneath thine own almighty wings."

I was eager to get to the fifth verse:

When in the night I sleepless lie, My soul with heav'nly thoughts supply;

Let no ill dreams disturb my rest, No powers of darkness me molest.[9]

I pretty much know many of the hymns in order, as well as most of the verses. I actually grew up in one of those families that gathered around the piano while Mom played and we all sang. Singing the hymns of the Church has been very formative of my faith and walk with our God—Father, Son, Spirit. I knew the hymn that came next, and I couldn't wait to sing it too:

Now rest beneath night's shadows the woodland, field and meadow; the world in slumber lies.

But you, my heart, awaking And prayer and music making, Let praise to your Creator rise.

It was verse four in this hymn that I was eager to sing:

Lord Jesus, since you love me, Now spread your wings above me And shield me from alarm.

Though Satan would devour me, Let angel guards sing o'er

me: This child of God shall meet no harm.[10]

I cannot explain exactly what happens in my mind and heart when I begin to sing, but when I began to sing the hymns that night, I found the grace, strength, and courage from Jesus that I needed. I am told that singing accesses more parts of the brain than reading or praying does, so singing touches us at a much deeper level. I find it powerful when I can sing prayers. It is strengthening to pray these, but to *sing* them touches me at an even deeper level. That night in the midst of being all alone in the desert, singing the hymns of the Church that have strengthened the people of God for generations was absolutely what brought peace to my soul. Singing aloud, and even singing some of the verses repeatedly, was how God brought peace to my soul.

Even the next day as the afternoon was nearly spent and I knew that the early darkness of that first week of January was near, I knew that I *had* the resource I needed to deal with the darkness and the fear. I had the hymns of the Church which had powerfully shaped my faith and life to that point, and they would again that second evening provide the recognition of the presence of Jesus that I needed. What gave me such grace and strength in the dark hours also led me to rise early before the sun came up. I would get up at first light, grab my hymnal again, and turn not to the Morning hymns, but to the Praise and Adoration section. As the sun rose over the Sierra Del Carmen Mountains in the east, I would sing with all the energy I could muster:

Alleluia! Let praises ring! To God the Father let us bring Our songs of adoration.[11]

When I sing alone, I can get stuck anywhere in the hymn and sing it again and again—"Our songs of adoration!" I love and am greatly strengthened by singing the hymns that contain an "Alleluia!"

Strengthened through Solitude with Jesus

This chapter is titled as it is because—after the Word and Sacraments of Worship--it is solitude, time with Jesus to meditate on His Word, and prayer in response that have become powerful patterns in my life. As a faithful Jewish rabbi, Jesus went regularly to the synagogue on the Sabbath. He led His disciples to do the same each Sabbath, and He used this as a time to teach and preach. Jesus also developed a pattern of solitude to be alone with the Father often, which continued to strengthen and empower Him for the mission the Father sent Him to accomplish.

Little has changed for us today. The worship on Sunday as we gather in community for our faith to be fed and strengthened by Word and Sacraments is vital and essential. Whether we want to talk about what is necessary for clergy or lay disciples of Jesus, it all begins with the worship on Sunday. Then, whether we want to talk about clergy or lay disciples of Jesus who want to live for and follow Him each day, like Jesus, we need to find a time and space to give God our undivided attention. Those of us who want to follow Jesus each day need Him to be "actively present in our lives—healing, teaching, and guiding" us in the way He wants us to go. Living for and following Jesus are not accidents. Living for and following Jesus require intentionally showing up and opening up to let Him shape, and mold, and use us as He chooses.

We also have choices. About eight years ago, two pastor friends of mine, one about six years younger and one about six years older, expressed the same intent. Each knew of my time in the desert of Big Bend, and each was anticipating a Sabbatical in the approaching summer. At the same conference in late January, each one said the very same thing to me in separate conversations. As they planned the activities of their summer leave, each one expressed, "I need to learn to get comfortable being alone with God!" Each of them was making the same confession that I had made about my reluctance to be alone with God. No one else needs to go spend a week in the desert of Big Bend at the "remote site" called Kbar. But each of us who wants to follow and be led by our Jesus needs to develop meaningful times and ways to be alone with Him.

As I look back at the first several weeks of my journal in the February of my "new reality," I see lots of uncertainty, confusion, questioning, pain, and honest wrestling with God in prayer. I also see Him providing hope, and strength, and peace, and encouragement for me to trust in Him and in the plans He was working out in my life. It is as if God has used these thirty-eight years of my life and ministry to prepare me to do this one difficult year of my life. Jesus has been schooling me to develop the pattern of "setting aside a time and place for God and him alone," so that He could continue His work of "healing, teaching, and guiding" me. The times of solitude with Him each day have sustained and strengthened me and provided the leading I have needed. I don't understand His fuller plan for my life yet, but I can see a number of the directions in which He is leading. He desires to be "actively present in our [my] lives—healing, teaching, and guiding." As I make the quiet space to be alone with Him, I experience Him restoring my soul and guiding my life.

Chapter Three: Questions for Reflection or Sharing

"Yet the news about him spread all the more so that crowds of people came to hear him and to be healed of their sicknesses. But Jesus often withdrew to lonely places and prayed." (Luke 5:15–16)

How comfortable are you being alone, especially being alone in solitude with Jesus?

Does Nouwen's assertion, "Without solitude it is virtually impossible to live a spiritual life," ring true for your journey of faith?

Do you consider solitude time alone with Jesus more important for full-time church workers than for lay followers of Jesus?

What is the longest period of solitude you have experienced, and where did you find it?

What has it been like for you to face your fear, and what gave you the courage to do so?

What are some hymns or songs of the faithful that God had used to strengthen you in fearful times?

CHAPTER FOUR

THE EXPERIENCE OF INJUSTICE

"You intended to harm me, but God intended it for good." (Genesis 50:20a)

Many people experience injustices in life that may come in many different forms: financial, relational, medical, and even the mental issues of dementia or Alzheimer's. In the course of living life, chances are good that each of us will experience at least one injustice. The issue is less the context of the injustice and more how one responds to it. A trust in the sovereignty of Jesus can provide a longer-range view of His plans and purposes for your life.

Really Hard Words to Hear

I hesitate even to mention the words again, because each time I do they stand as the same shocking reality! "The Board has voted unanimously to go in a different direction in the position of senior pastor." I know that these words were very difficult words for me to hear, and I think they were very difficult words for the Board to speak. I believe that they were difficult words to speak, because several Board members sought to affirm me on the heels of their announced decision, "But we love you, and respect you, and appreciate everything you have done." I do not know the deliberations that went into their decision; I only know what they voted unanimously to do.

At a subsequent meeting, I suggested those words of affirmation did not logically follow their unanimous vote. It's much like two people who are married, and then one makes a decision and says, "We are getting a divorce!" The words that follow that announcement will not be, "But I love you, and respect you, and appreciate you." To that, two Board members responded quickly, "But we do love you and respect you, and you are the reason our family is at this church!"

This is the reason I think these were difficult words for the Board members to speak. The words sent an inconsistent message to me, but they were repeated a second time, so I still struggle to find their truth. The best I can do is to try to understand them in the context of another message from a Board member, when only four of us were present. I believe he said truthfully, "Walt, don't take this personally. It's not personal; it's just a business decision. I hope in several years we will be able to sit together and share an iced tea." It all continues to be a bit bewildering.

A Biblical Story of Injustice

I don't know how you read and understand the story of Joseph and his brothers as it begins in Genesis 37. Joseph, at the age of seventeen, wearing his richly-adorned robe, was his father's favorite—which is saying something in a family of twelve sons. It is hard to say how much Jacob contributed to the problem and how much was sibling rivalry and jealousy among the brothers. God had certainly gifted Joseph with the ability to interpret dreams, which enraged his brothers and turned them against him even more. At one point, even his father rebuked Joseph for his dreams. The brothers eventually wanted to kill him, but the oldest brother, Reuben, sought to save his life. Finally, they sold Joseph into slavery to a caravan of Ishmaelites.

From this point on, the Joseph story definitely becomes one of injustice. Potiphar, an official of the Pharaoh in Egypt, bought Joseph from the Ishmaelites. Joseph became a source of great blessing for Potiphar, so much so that Potiphar eventually put Joseph in charge of everything in his household. Joseph lived and worked for Potiphar in the most honest and trustworthy manner. This was especially true when Potiphar's wife tried to seduce this "well-built and handsome man" (Genesis 39:6). Joseph did the honorable thing and refused her advances by saying, "How then could I do such a wicked thing and sin against God?" (Genesis 39:9). Unfortunately, Potiphar believed his lying wife, and Joseph was thrown into prison where he was an honorable prisoner.

Even while Joseph was in prison, God was with him and enabled word to get to Pharaoh that Joseph could interpret dreams. Joseph did so for the Pharaoh and became the second-most powerful ruler in all of Egypt. He was put in charge of the kingdom and of storing the food surplus from the seven years of plenty to supply the seven years of famine. The famine was experienced even in Israel, a circumstance which brought the sons of Jacob to Egypt and in contact with the brother whom they did not now recognize. But Joseph recognized them and could not resist the opportunity to "mess with them" just a bit. He caused no great problems for them, but he did seem to get some joy from "messing with them" just a bit.

Eventually Joseph made himself known to his brothers and had a wonderful reunion with his father when the whole family moved to Egypt. Only after their father died years later were they afraid that Joseph would now have his revenge. Joseph responded to reassure them:

"Don't be afraid. Am I in the place of God? You intended it to harm me, but God intended it for good to accomplish what is now being done, the saving of many lives" (Genesis 50:19–20).

Defining Injustice

It is easier for us to define injustice in the second half of the Joseph story when he was in Egypt. Joseph was honorable and trustworthy and did only the right thing. Nevertheless, he ended up in prison. A lying wife turned the tables, and Potiphar was enraged without justification, since Joseph had been trustworthy in every way in Potiphar's house.

In relational conflict, it is not always as easy to define justice. This is especially so in a church disagreements when prayers are said and people believe they are being led by God; it gets confusing. One thing I know in my situation is that I did none of those things that the church stipulates are reasons for removing a pastor. Everyone agrees that I did not teach or preach false doctrine. I was not involved in any scandalous behavior. I embezzled no money from the church. I was not involved in those things that provide grounds for removing a pastor. Therefore, I am left to think that the fault was that I was not the business-oriented pastor that they wanted. Even at that, what they did, and the way in which they did it, was an injustice to me and many in this Church Family.

From the first morning after the Board shared their decision with me, as I prayed, "Jesus give me a heart like yours," He began to create a different spirit in me. The anger and the anxiety I kept expecting to feel did not come. Instead, Jesus gave me a spirit that responded, "Lots of people experience injustice in the world, so how arrogant would I be to claim my life should be exempt from injustice." I can only believe this came from Jesus, because I have never before thought this thought. I have been more inclined to fight injustice where I see it. Now that I was the object of the injustice in a way I had never been before, Jesus gave me a spirit to respond, "Lots of people experience injustice, and how arrogant would I be to claim my life should be exempt from injustice."

One good friend recently told me, "I don't know the details, and I don't need to know the details. I know you, and I know that you got bushwhacked!" This friend is not originally from Texas, but he has been in Texas long enough to use a Texas way of saying what happened: "I know that you got bushwhacked!" It became obvious to me that many others also felt that I got bushwhacked, because they came up and wanted to tell me their stories of injustice.

The first was an aircraft mechanic who said, "They sold off all my airplanes, and they sold me off too!"

Another said, "I was fifty-seven when the governor of Texas decided to do some cost-cutting and got rid of my job. I had no transferrable skills to work elsewhere."

An international missionary called from the upper Midwest to say, "I was sixty-four years old when my Board called me in to say that I was going to retire!"

A pastor from another denomination told me that sixteen years ago his Board let him go, because they said he "was preaching too much Scripture!"

Another friend said, "They decided to cut cost, so they just cut my job. Then, what was worse, they put lies in my file!"

Another missionary friend who now lives in Colorado said, "They didn't just kick me out of a church after twelve years; they kicked me out of a whole country!"

Another man told me he had been an architect until one Sunday afternoon his friend and Christian boss said, "You don't work here anymore."

Many people experience real injustice in the world. It happens outside the church and inside the church. The more stories from others that I heard, the more I began to understand the reason that God had indeed planted that thought in my mind and heart, "How arrogant would I be to claim that my life should be exempt from injustice."

A local friend, whose parents live in New Mexico, shared my situation with them. After they heard my story, they sent him a copy of a letter called "From the desk of Father George." Father George is a Dominican priest who, with his Dominican brothers, had been removed from their ministry. This is a small part of his response to being let go: "All of us will—in time—recover. That recovery begins with the forgiveness Jesus has told us to beg of God. And it is within that forgiveness that love will lead us to go forward. But right now I am not ashamed of my rage. The thought of going gently is not yet completely with me. But it too will come."

Responding to Injustice

Some have asked me, "Why don't we *fight* this?" Another good friend said, "We need to mount an offensive and go after the Board!" My response was that I was not inclined to do that for two reasons. First, I could not imagine how a public fight would be good for this Church Family. Second, it was not what Jesus was leading me to do. It is significant that on the same February 14 journal entry when I first wrote, "Why should I be exempt from injustice?" I also have the names of the nine Board members for whom I prayed that morning.

It was on Thursday, February 20 that I wrote in my journal, "I will need to stay with Romans 12:9–21, as You have much to teach me in these verses." These were difficult and challenging words for me, especially during this period. This journal entry came just over a week after I shared with the congregation what the Board had decided and my response to their decision, which was to retire on June 29. Romans 12 was the Epistle Lesson the very next Sunday. I was not preaching, but

I did lead the prayers during worship, and thus wrestled mightily with these verses. The complete context is available to read, but here are the verses that jumped out at me:

> v9–10: "Love must be sincere. Hate what is evil; cling to what is good. Be devoted to one another in brotherly love. Honor one another above yourselves" (Romans 12).

> v14: "Bless those who persecute you; bless and do not curse" (Romans 12).

> v17: "Do not repay anyone evil for evil. Be careful to do what is right in the eyes of everybody" (Romans 12).

> v21: "Do not be overcome by evil, but overcome evil with good" (Romans 12).

Paul seems to be echoing Jesus' words from Luke, as He encouraged those who follow Him: "But I tell you who hear me: Love your enemies, do good to those who hate you, bless those who curse you, pray for those who mistreat you" (Luke 6:27–28).

Whether I looked at the words of Paul or of Jesus, these verses were disconcerting for me, because the instructions they offer were not my natural inclination. It was difficult to follow this scriptural encouragement. To think of how to love these people, honor them, and bless them was not what I wanted to invest my energies in doing, especially in relation to the Board. I didn't believe that the Board had persecuted me. I did feel that they had publicly dishonored, mistreated, and been disrespectful to me, but they had not persecuted me.

Seeking a Way to Bless Them

Even though the Board had not officially persecuted me, I still could not ignore these verses. I still had to struggle with a way to bless them. I absolutely did not want to bless them, but if I wanted to follow Jesus, I had to wrestle with this. *How* in the world could I bless them? I wrestled with this again and again, and then I knew the answer. Because of my brokenness with the Board, it was becoming very difficult for me to give them the Sacrament. As I wrestled with this situation, I began to believe that there was a clear and specific way for me to bless them. I would give them the Sacrament, which is a major blessing to them. In the midst of struggling to make sense of this confusing, bewildering, and crazy situation, there was one thing that was very clear. I could seek to bless them by giving them the Sacrament. What more significant way to bless them than with the Sacrament that Jesus Himself gave?

I could also bless them by continuing to pray for them. Jesus clearly says to "pray for those who mistreat you." Jesus Himself did so in the very worst circumstances of all, and He calls us to do the same. I must admit that very soon after this happened, I did pray for them the prayer of Jesus from the cross: "Father, forgive them, for they do not know what they are doing" (Luke 23:34). I prayed it with more of an emphasis on the second half of that prayer, "for they do not know what they are doing." I didn't think they had the slightest clue what they were doing. Then I had to shift to focus more on the first half, "Father, forgive them."

My prayers later changed to ones of blessing for them, for those who had mistreated me. These are difficult and challenging prayers to pray, but that is precisely what Jesus encourages us to do. I told a counselor friend of mine shortly after my last Sunday on June 29, 2014, "I want to delete the nine names of the Board from the phone list in my cell phone. I want to go delete, delete, delete." That is what I wanted to do, but I don't think that is what Jesus would want me to do. I think that Jesus would want me to keep them in their alphabetical arrangement, and each time I see one of their names to use it as a reminder to pray a blessing for that person. It is still difficult and challenging for me to see those names, but they are my intentional reminder to pray blessings for them.

While it still isn't exactly easy to do, I am finding it helpful to be able to take the longer-range view of the whole Joseph story from Genesis 37–50. It is a wonderful reminder that God in His sovereignty had a clear plan and purpose that He was working out, even in the midst of the petty jealousy of the brothers. God was still sovereign and at work, even in spite of a seductive and lying wife and the unjust rage of her husband who had been greatly blessed by God because of Joseph. God was sovereign, even from an Egyptian prison, to move Joseph to become the second highest in command, the right hand of the Pharaoh in Egypt. *And* God is still sovereign in my life, working out His plans and purposes to use me in the ways He intends. I need to learn to *trust* and *rely* on Him.

Many people are discovering the daily devotional, *Jesus Calling,* by Sarah Young. The devotion for May 7th includes Joseph and has Jesus encouraging, "If you learn to trust Me—really trust Me—with your whole being, then nothing can separate you from My Peace. Everything you endure can be put to good use by allowing it to train you in trusting Me. This is how you foil the works of evil, growing in grace through the very adversity that was meant to harm you. Joseph was a prime example of this divine reversal, declaring to his brothers: 'You meant evil against me, but God meant it for good.' . . . Do not fear what this day, or any day, may bring your way. Concentrate on trusting Me and doing what needs to be done. Relax in My sovereignty, remembering that I go before you, as well as with you, into each day. Fear no evil, for I can bring good out of every situation you will encounter".[12]

Chapter Four: Questions for Reflection or Sharing

"You intended it to harm me, but God intended it for good." (Genesis 50:20a).

Other than the story of Joseph, what are some other biblical stories of injustice of which you are aware?

Do you have a story of personal injustice or know of others from family or friends?

How do you make sense out of a church disagreement where both sides have prayed and believe they are right and doing what God is calling them to do?

Have you ever wrestled with Jesus' words, "pray for those who mistreat you," in relation to someone who has wronged you? If so, what was that like?

Is there a situation in which you need to take a longer-range view of God's sovereignty to work for good?

Is there a situation in which you need to imagine Jesus saying, "Relax in my sovereignty, remembering that I go before you, as well as with you, into each day"?[13]

SHARING THE NEWS: "LET GO OF THE BRANCH!"

*"But this I call to mind, and therefore I have hope: The steadfast love of the L*ORD *never ceases, his mercies never come to an end; they are new every morning; great is thy faithfulness. 'The L*ORD *is my portion,' says my soul, 'therefore I will hope in him.'" (Lamentations 3:21–24, RSV)*

"Faith is a living, daring confidence in God's grace, so sure and certain that a man would stake his life on it a thousand times."

—Martin Luther, Commentary on Romans

Each of us faces defining or pivotal moments in life. Often those moments lead us in a completely different direction than we had ever planned. Most often, it means letting go of the future you had seen for yourself. There is a letting go of the future you planned and a willingness to let Jesus take you wherever *He* chooses. Such letting go can only be done with a trust that the future toward which Jesus is leading you is far better than anything you had envisioned.

Going Public with "My New Reality"

After almost two weeks of wrestling with the Board's decision and prayerfully weighing what my response to it should be, next came the task of letting this Church Family know about the changes that were coming. I needed to find a gracious way to let them know that my decision was a response to the decision that the Board made "to go in a different direction in the position of senior pastor." I discovered that some implications established by our insurance and retirement plans meant that I either had to work until I was sixty-six or retire by June 30, 2014. I was going to be only sixty-four on February 27, 2014, so I chose to retire on June 30.

I sought to be honest, and gracious, and hopeful. Before I could share hope with this Church Family, I had to find it myself. I don't know what others do, but I find that I can't fake hope! If I do not have it, I cannot share it, especially under the difficult circumstances in which I found myself. Along with Romans 15:13, one of the most significant verses of hope from the Word of God for me has long been Lamentations 3:21ff. Those who had been in this Church Family for some time had heard me share these verses on numerous occasions, and they knew of the hope I gain from them.

On that weekend, I shared at each worship service what the Board had decided, my response which was to retire, and about how I still had HOPE. I knew so little about what the future held, but I chose to move forward, trusting that God had a plan. I told them that I had way too much energy and passion for Jesus, and because of that, I was sure that He still had a plan and purpose for my life. The truth was that I could see almost none of that plan and purpose, but I still chose to trust Jesus.

During other times in my life after I came out of a difficult period,

I have had to say to Jesus, "I could not begin to imagine how in the world You could possibly bring good out of that mess, so I did not trust You. Next time I have a chance, I want to trust You, even when I can't see what You are doing or how You are at work for good!" Without a doubt, this was *one* of those "next times." In fact, I don't think I have ever experienced a time when I could see less of the future and had to trust Jesus more. My primary connection to Jesus has always been the Word of God!

The Necessity of the Word of God for Followers of Jesus

I have always loved teaching the Crossways course, which was developed by an Australian Lutheran pastor named Harry Wendt. This course is a two-year overview of the Bible from Genesis to Revelation. In four fifteen-week semesters, a class can systematically walk through the entire biblical narrative. Each of the eight times that I've taught Crossways, there has always been something new to learn. I absolutely believe that until the day Jesus takes me home, there will always be something new for me to learn from the Word of God.

From my perspective, there are two different ways to approach God's Word: for information and for formation. Neither way of approaching the Word is exclusive of the other; each overlaps the other. Yet each provides a distinct and important function in the life of a disciple of Jesus. Without both, the journey of a disciple of Jesus is diminished. We need the informational approach, and we need the formational approach.

The informational approach seems to come first. It is not exclusive, but we need to get to know our God and how He relates and responds to His people. It's important to get to know people like Abraham, Jacob, Moses, Deborah, Gideon, David, Jeremiah, Matthew, Peter, Paul, and

Silas and how God called, changed, and used their lives. The more deeply I get to know them, the more deeply I begin to understand God and His calling, changing, and using my life. I need to read and study the stories that are such a rich part of the biblical narrative. Getting to know the people of the Word of God enables me to learn about them and especially about Him. The more I know about how He related and responded to them, the more I will know about how He will relate and respond to me.

Second, and equally as important, is the formational approach. The Word of God is not designed only to fill my head with knowledge, as important as that function is in the life of each follower of Jesus. If I don't read and study His Word, my ideas about God will be only the fabrication of my own brain. That is a very weak substitute for the power of the Word. As important as the information is, I *must* also let the Word of God affect my heart and my life. God's Word is also designed to form, mold, and shape me to live my life to follow Jesus.

Once I come to faith in Jesus as my Savior, once I begin to accept by faith the incredible grace of God in the cross and resurrection of Jesus, the rest of my life is lived to follow Jesus. The more I learn to follow Jesus faithfully, the more He changes my heart and life to enable me to live more like Him.

Jesus' objective with each of His followers is to work in us by His Spirit to shape and form us to become more like Him so that increasingly we respond to others as Jesus would. Others begin to experience the grace and love of Jesus through us, and they are drawn to Him.

I absolutely love to sing the simple prayer song by Daniel Iverson called "Spirit of the Living God" about how the Spirit of Jesus continues His work to transform, fill, and use me. From the point of accepting by faith God's incredible grace in Jesus, the rest of my life is intended to be lived to follow Jesus faithfully as one of His disciples. In the same way that Jesus specifically called the twelve to follow Him, so He specifically calls everyone who has accepted Him as their Savior to follow Him.

I sometimes wonder whether all those who believe in Jesus as their Savior actually know that He has not just called them to believe in Him. That is the first step that He works in us so that, with the hands of a beggar, by faith we accept all He has already done for us. He never intended for anyone just to believe in Him. He called people to follow Him and to become increasingly more like Him. From now until Jesus returns or calls me home, I am to follow Him and be open to the work of His Spirit to mature me to become more like Him. If I do not, I will stay a baby follower who has little or no effect on others or on the world.

Drawing Grace and Strength from the Word

I know that by teaching Crossways I have systematically walked through the biblical narrative at least eight times. That does not include other teaching, or preaching, or reading of Scripture. I would only be guessing to try to say which cycle of Crossways led me really to see for the first time the powerful words of hope in Lamentations 3:21ff. I suspect that I am not the first person to read a passage repeatedly and then suddenly one day to see the words almost literally jump off the page. I had pondered these words before, but this particular time, they had a depth, and meaning, and hope that I had never experienced.

The book of Lamentations is not normally the first place one would go for hope and strength. The book is mainly just what the title says— Laments! The very first verse sets the tone: "How deserted lies the city, once so full of people! How like a widow is she, who once was great among the nations! She who was queen among the provinces has now become a slave" (Lamentations 1:1, RSV). Or consider verse 11 of the first chapter: "All her people groan as they search for bread; they barter their treasures for food to keep themselves alive. Look, O LORD, and consider, for I am despised!" (1:11).

This is difficult and painful stuff to read, and there are five more chapters of this depressing material. The children of Israel had turned their backs on God, refused to listen to His prophets, and now they were in exile. Exile is miserable, and they were miserable! The information in the book of Lamentations defines the reality of existence in exile away from the city of Jerusalem that now lay in ruins. How were the Israelites to find hope and strength and grace from God?

Amazingly, right in the middle of the most depressing book in the Bible is a most extraordinary passage of hope. This is when the formational approach becomes so vital. We hold onto God by these words of hope in Him and by His love and His faithfulness to us. It's always about God, and not about us. It's always about holding onto God and the hope and love that only He can provide! I hold onto God's faithfulness that is new every morning! I say to myself, "'The LORD is my portion,' says my soul, 'therefore I will hope in him'" (Lamentations 3:24, RSV). I say it repeatedly, and I pray it repeatedly, until He enables me to begin to believe it. I pray it repeatedly until He uses it to change my heart by the hope He plants there. I still can't see what He is doing or even sense it, but I will hope and trust and rely on *Him* to figure it out and then to lead the way.

I never set out to memorize these verses, but I have gone back to them so many times that they just became part of me. I prayed them again and again, and I pleaded them again and again. That is how these verses have grown to be one of my most significant passages of hope. They have become such a part of me that I can say or pray the words, wherever I happen to be. These verses calm my spirit when I need it during the day. I can pray them at night when I lie in bed unable to get to sleep. I have shared these verses countless times with others who needed a major encouragement of *hope*. Having hope and knowing in whom you find it are basic to our human existence. Without hope, we give up.

The Wrestling before the Sharing

In my journal entry on Saturday, February 15, 2014, I wrote, "Let go of the branch! Okay, okay, okay, I will let go of the branch. I am letting go of the branch. *You* know how much I need *You* today and tomorrow. I will trust and rely on *You* alone for all I need. Stay with me, Jesus, and be my great surprise. *You* have been the one who has carried me these past several weeks, and I am sure that *You* will be the One who provides all I need in these days. *You* are the God of Hope, full of Joy and Peace as I Trust in *You*. Jesus, carry me."

This was the weekend I would share my "new reality." I had never walked this way before in thirty-eight-plus years, so I had no idea quite how this would go. What I would do was point this Church Family to the hope I had in the God who had always been faithful. I would tell them of the Jesus who had been, and I am sure would continue, carrying me in the midst of this situation. I would call them to join me to trust the Jesus we follow.

I would say to them that to trust God was to "Let go of the branch!" Maybe you've heard the old story about "Jack" who was walking one day too close to a cliff's edge and fell. He grabbed onto a branch on the way down and cried out, "Help! Help!" He listens, but there is no response. So he prays for God to help him. God then answers in a large, emphatic voice: "Let go of the branch!" Jack thinks for a minute and then asks, "Is there anybody else up there?"

Let Go of the Branch!

As clearly, specifically, and as plainly as I could say it, that was what I was doing. I was "Letting Go of the Branch." I had many more questions than answers, but I also had a firm conviction that God was telling me to "Let Go!" I actually did tell this Church Family that very thing: "I have far too much energy and passion for Jesus for Him to leave me sitting on the sidelines." I felt sure that He would continue to make use of my life and gifts in ways that I was yet to discover. With that trust, I would move forward, relying on Jesus to lead the way.

I have lived and prayed and journaled these words of Galatians: "I have been crucified with Christ and I no longer live, but Christ lives in me. The life I live in the body, I live by faith in the Son of God, who loved me and gave himself for me" (Galatians 2:20). I have held onto these words, and wondered, and wrestled with exactly what Paul meant by, "I no longer live, but Christ lives in me." Now I was beginning to understand that when I don't know, when I can't see the way, when I can't even imagine what may need to happen next—I need to let go and let Jesus take charge. "I no longer live, but Christ lives in me." I know without a doubt that He loves me and gave His life for me, so I will, in fact, trust that "Christ lives in me." And I will let Him take charge and do whatever He knows is best.

I have never been so dependent on Jesus, I have never so fully reliant on Jesus, I have never been so carried by Jesus! At first, it was a bit scary, but then it was powerfully strengthening. Since Jesus is living in me and Jesus is in charge of my life, it absolutely could not get any better than this. I knew so little of what was about to happen, but I knew by faith and trusted the *One* who was leading me, and I knew that He is absolutely faithful!

I recall another very familiar Scripture passage that many followers of Jesus seek to live by and to trust. Many have memorized it, perhaps because they have gone back to it again and again: "And we know that in all things God works for the good of those who love him, who have been called according to his purpose" (Romans 8:28). What a profound promise God makes, that even in the midst of the greatest difficulty, we can *know* He is always at work for good! It seems that Paul may also have taken the longer-range view of things and events. Knowing that God in His sovereignty always has a plan that He is working out for the good of those who love Him, Paul encourages us to trust God to be good.

Not everyone knows the two verses that precede verse 28; I knew that verse long before I ever discovered verses 26–27. Sometimes before we get to the good God is working as He promised, we have to go through some of the confusion, and bewilderment, and pain of verses 26–27: "In the same way, the Spirit helps us in our weakness. We do not know what we ought to pray for, but the Spirit himself intercedes for us with groans that words cannot express. And he who searches our hearts knows the mind of the Spirit, because the Spirit intercedes for the saints in accordance with God's will." God always is at work for good, but He is also always honest with us. Before we get to the good that He is working for us, there will also be the reality of our weakness, and confusion, and bewilderment, and pain.

We can teach our God nothing about pain. The Father who gave up His one and only Son and Jesus who suffered the pain and abandonment of the cross—they can teach us about pain. In the midst of our pain is when the Spirit of Jesus prays for us. How absolutely incredible is that! When we are weak, when we don't know where things are going next, when we don't even know what we need to pray for—*that* is precisely when the Spirit of Jesus Himself prays for us.

It is both a difficult place to be—not even to know what we need to pray for—and greatly strengthening to know that the Spirit prays for us at just such times. We can't even begin to understand this higher-level prayer conversation, because the Spirit prays for us "with groans that words cannot express." The great news is that when the Spirit prays for us, He always prays "for the saints in accordance with God's will," and that means that His prayers are always very good!

A Precarious and Promising Place to Be

I have been in some very difficult places in my life, but I don't know that I have ever quite had to "Let Go of the Branch" like this. On the one hand, not knowing where the ground is or when you might get there is a precarious place to be. On the other hand, it is a place of powerful promise to be where Jesus is leading and guiding every step. Sarah Young's devotional, *Jesus Calling*, expresses some of the promises I found in imagining Jesus to say, "Come to me and rest. I am all around you to bless and restore. Breathe me in with every breath. The way ahead of you is very steep. Slow down and cling tightly to my hand. I am teaching you a difficult lesson learned only by hardship".[14]

Perhaps because of my cartoon, imagining Jesus saying the following meant even more: "Be willing to go out on a limb with me. If that is where I am leading you, it is the safest place to be. In order to follow me wholeheartedly, you must relinquish your tendency to play it safe. Eventually, you will learn to relax and enjoy the adventure of our journey together".[15] Not only did I feel like I was out on the limb with Jesus but I was also letting go of the limb, which I believed Jesus was leading me to do. One of the verses Sarah Young cites in this same devotion is from the familiar 23rd Psalm: "Even though I walk through the valley of the shadow of death, I will fear no evil, for you are with me; your rod and your staff, they comfort me" (Psalm 23:4).

It didn't feel like I was approaching death, but I prayed that the Lord would enable me to "fear no evil" in the darkness in which I was living. I was very sure that I wanted to "enjoy the adventure of our journey together." When our daughters were growing up, my job on family vacations was always to "find an adventure" wherever we happened to be. So this word "adventure" made me smile when I read it. It was a good thing to think about the weeks and months ahead when I did not know exactly where this was going, to think of it all as an "adventure" with something new to discover around the next corner. It definitely made me more hopeful to approach this period with the attitude of seeking the "adventure" in it all.

A Living, Daring Confidence!

Dr. Martin Luther, in his preface to his *Commentary on the Book of Romans*, boldly affirmed, "Faith is a living, daring confidence in God's grace, so sure and certain a man would stake his life on it a thousand times." I love that word *confidence*, which for me goes so well with faith and trust. Confidence generally has to do with one's own feeling of certainty that he will succeed. Luther leaves no room for self-confidence, but places any focus of confidence squarely on God's grace. Luther affirms, as no one else could, that faith in our amazing God enables us to move forward with a "living, daring confidence in God's grace." So faith is a confidence always in our God of grace.

A particular hymn verse is always attached to the word confidence for me.

> *If you but trust in God to guide you And place your confidence in him, You'll find him always there beside you To give you hope and strength with-in. For those who trust God's changeless love Build on the rock that will not move.*[16]

Luther affirms the only one in whom we can "place our confidence" is our God and His grace. As I place my confidence in Him, I find that He is always there to provide the hope and strength I need, precisely when I need it.

CHAOS TO HOPE TO HEALING

This whole affirmation is said with the strong conviction that only Luther would risk. This one who literally put his life on the line for the sake of his beliefs about Jesus and the gospel would not affirm this lightly. He says that this faith is "so sure and certain a man would stake his life on it a thousand times." Either Luther is the major master of overstatement or he wants very, very emphatically to emphasize the strength of his conviction.

One might say that there is an overabundance of faith on which a man (or woman) would be ready to stake his or her life—not fifty times, nor one hundred times, nor two hundred times, nor five hundred times, nor six hundred-fifty times, nor eight hundred-fifty times, *but* 1000 times! I discovered this Luther quote only two years ago. In these last two years, God has used it as I have held onto confidence in His grace to make my faith more living and daring.

Chapter Five: Questions for Reflection or Sharing

"Faith is a living, daring confidence in God's grace, so sure and certain that a man would stake his life on it a thousand times." (Martin Luther)

Think about a time when you had to move forward without knowing what the future held, but you were trusting that God had a plan.

As you approach the Word of God for information, where might you need to spend more time in study?

As you approach the Word of God for formation, what are some of the verses you need to hold onto so that the Spirit of Jesus might change or work to shape you?

Is there a situation about which you need to pray repeatedly, "Therefore I will hope in him," until God plants hope in your heart?

Has there been a time when you had to "let go of the branch" and simply trust God? Do you need to do so at this time?

If you could find the "living, daring confidence in God's grace" of which Luther speaks, what might you be led to do?

CHAPTER SIX

STAYING CURRENT IN RELATIONSHIP WITH JESUS FOR DIRECTION

"Remain in me, and I will remain in you. No branch can bear fruit by itself; it must remain in the vine. Neither can you bear fruit unless you remain in me." (John 15:4)

"Live in me. Make your home in me just as I do in you. In the same way that a branch can't bear grapes by itself but only by being joined to the vine, you can't bear fruit unless you are joined to me." (John 15:4, The Message)

The Word of God is *the* source of faith and practice as we follow Jesus. The Word is the way Jesus continues to shape, and form, and strengthen our faithfulness in following Him. Some of our life questions of Jesus are not answered directly in the Word. Some of our life questions—such as about job changes, house moves, what to do in relationships with growing children, or aging parents in memory care, are discerned more with Jesus' guidance. The Word will always strengthen our relationship with Jesus, so He can provide the direction we need.

We Have to Spend Our Time on the Water

I love to fish—your boat or my boat or a guide's boat, fresh water or saltwater, inshore or offshore—you name the time and the place, and I'll be there! We can fish for striper, hybrids, or sand bass; for northern, walleye, or small mouth; for speckled trout, redfish, or flounder; for sailfish, dorado, tuna, or marlin! I grew up fishing mainly in saltwater with my dad and grandpa, but thirty-eight years in Fort Worth led to more freshwater fishing. I just talked with my son-in-law about taking him and my grandson to Texoma where they are catching some good striper. I love to fish! By the grace of God and the good will of several fishing buddies, I have probably already caught more than my fair share of the world's fish. As long as I am able, I will keep fishing!

I have learned three things about fishing that need to happen if I hope to catch fish regularly. First, some basic fishing knowledge and some fishing success are crucial. These usually come from fishing with someone with significant fishing experience. Fishermen are usually good-natured people, and they are glad to take someone along and show him the basics about what rods and reels to get, what line to use, what the basic lures to begin with are, and how to use them all successfully. Success generally begins with a fishing buddy who is ready to help others learn.

Second, it really helps to develop a good network of fishing buddies who are willing to share information about the lake. It's always helpful to know where they have been catching the fish, what time of day was best, and which lures they were using. About thirty years ago, a friend and I began fishing together in a fifteen-foot aluminum boat with a seven-and-one-half horsepower Sears outboard motor that my cousin was glad to loan us. Most Saturdays, a couple at church named Ken and Vera would go fishing at Lake Grapevine. On Sunday in a brief meeting in the hallway, they were happy to tell me where they had caught their fish, what time of day it was, and the lures that were hottest. Monday was my day off, and more often than not, we were successful because of the hot tip of the day before. A network for obtaining current information is very helpful.

Third, time has to be spent on the water. Trust me on this one. I don't care how many times a person has fished a lake, if that person hasn't been on the water for six weeks, there will be disorientation, and it takes a little while to get one's bearings straight. If a person has been on the lake regularly for the past three weeks, there will be a game plan for the best places to fish, and those can be ranked one, two, and three. Time on the water is so valuable, because a person learns how to ask the right questions of others who are fishing nearby, even if they are strangers. There is nothing more important than time on the water! The reality is that nothing is more important for the Christian than spending time daily with our God—Father, Son, Spirit. Even if things are currently going well in life, still nothing is more important than spending time with God.

Spend Plenty of Time with God!

My journal is simply a book of blank pages. A spiral notebook has often worked just as well for me as a fancier journal. On the bottom of every right-hand page, for at least the last five years, I have always written the same quotation from Oswald Chambers as a way to keep me intentional and disciplined about my morning solitude with God. It reads: "Spend plenty of time with God, let other things go, But Do Not neglect Him!" The capitalization "But Do Not" is my emphasis, because I need the reminder.

Over twenty-five years ago we wanted to encourage everyone in our Church Family to practice daily times of solitude. To encourage this practice, we made up a bright red sticker with white letters that read: "Spend some time with God today." If I had known the Chambers' quotation back then, I would probably have included the word "plenty." Throughout those same twenty-five years, a good number of men have said, "I don't do bumper stickers, but give me one of those!" These stickers are now seen on boats, pickups, Bibles, backpacks, refrigerators, bathroom mirrors, and other creative places. Everyone knows it's a great encouragement for all.

When I have those periods in my life when I've slipped off-track and have not made the time for solitude, I subtly begin to act as if I am in charge of my life. I generally would not have admitted it; I would have instead rationalized that I believe in Jesus and think I have a pretty good idea of what He wants me to do with my life. I am probably okay for a while by myself, and I excuse myself by saying that I will get back on track with the solitude soon. I may rock along pretty well for a while and fend pretty well for myself. However, eventually a difficulty will wake me up or a crisis will slap me around, and I will come to my senses. The reality for each of us every day is that nothing is more important than spending plenty of time with God!

Please know that solitude with God does not shield or protect us from difficulty or crisis. When I learned of "my new reality" in January of 2014, I had been experiencing just over a year of significant spiritual growth. My workload had increased because of some staff vacancies, we were in the process of calling others to staff, and my trust and reliance on Jesus were at a high point. I continued to pray that Jesus would give me the wisdom and courage I needed to lead. After I learned that the Board had "voted to go another direction," I began to have the feeling that everything in my life had prepared me for this crisis period. My reliance on God was strong, but I knew it would need to increase. By December of 2014, I do believe that everything in my life had prepared me to endure this crisis and to thrive.

Discovering Grace, Strength, and Courage

A close friend recently went through a very difficult crisis in his family because of a prolonged hospitalization of a family member. We have been close for many years, but because of a move to another state, we haven't seen each other so much in the last several years. He had been very faithful in following Jesus and in his times of prayer and solitude with God. More recently, it seemed that other things had gotten in the way and had taken priority. He had gotten off-track a bit, though I am sure he still believed in Jesus as his Savior.

In the midst of this crisis, I watched Jesus bring him back so much closer. I remember well the day he told me that he had not been reading and praying the prayers of John Baillie each day, but now he was so glad to be back to them. I also noted the call when he told me of singing again each day the words from the song "Spirit of the Living God" and how it was strengthening him. I listened over the weeks as we spoke regularly on the phone, and heard how Jesus brought him so much closer again. I kept thinking of the words of encouragement from James: "Come near to God and He will come near to you" (James 4:7). Jesus always initiates, gently nudging us back toward Him, and He will always welcome us back.

This is exactly the reason that nothing is more important than spending time with our God. If I haven't spent time with Him lately, it leaves me disoriented and it takes me a while to get my bearings. If I haven't spent time with God in the past several months, when a crisis happens, I lack a game plan of how to proceed. If I have been spending time with God, the grace, strength, and courage I need are readily available.

The rest of what I have discovered will make less sense until you actually begin to personally explore solitude with Jesus. I shared earlier the pattern of Jesus' life and His priority for solitude with the Father. Quite frankly, every Sunday is intended to be a time to slow the pace, and quiet the noise, and rest. John Baillie has a prayer for the morning and evening of each day of the month and a morning and evening prayer for Sunday. These three sentences from his prayer for Sunday morning have long been salutary for me: "Give me grace for such an act of self-recollection as may again bring together the scattered forces of my soul. Enable me to step aside for a little while from the busy life of common days and take thought about its meaning and its end. May Jesus Christ be today the companion of my thoughts, so that His Spirit may more and more take root within my soul".[17]

Everyone needs these times that Baillie leads us to pray for to "step aside from the busy life of common days." I can actually remember when I was growing up in the 1950s and 1960s that Sundays really were more of a Sabbath or a day that was different from the other days of the week. Especially in Texas where "blue laws" kept stores from opening for business on Sunday, it could be a time to take a break. Now, Sunday is very much like the other six days; so few people "step aside" so that Jesus can "bring together the scattered forces of my soul." The grace, strength, and courage are readily available to me, but without the solitude with Jesus, I keep His Spirit from "more and more taking root within my soul."

Disciples Need Rest with Jesus

About twenty years ago some friends let us use a condominium on South Padre Island near the very southern tip of Texas. I distinctly remember walking into that condominium where one of the first things I saw was a plaque that invited and encouraged us to, "Rest, Relax, Renew, Restore, Re-generate." I left the plaque on the wall, but I took all the R-words with me. They continue to be a great encouragement for me to slow the pace, quiet the noise, and sit quietly at Jesus' feet. As I am writing this, I am in a home of friends near Rockport, just north of Padre Island. Here is another plaque that greets me with these words of encouragement: "RELAX—how beautiful it is to do nothing and rest afterwards."

Most of us modern, high achievers are really, really uncomfortable "doing nothing." It drives us crazy to sit and do nothing. We are able to sit in front of a television for hours, focused on our favorite sporting event, but to be in a quiet place without something to do is unnerving. Not only do most of us need something to do, we also often need to be "multi-tasking" or else we feel or fear that we are just wasting time. "Rest, Relax, Renew" are simply words that are not in our vocabulary. Our pattern is more to seek to maximize our every minute to get the most out of every day!

The story of Mary and Martha in Luke 10 has long made me feel uncomfortable. I had a grandmother named Martha who was very well typecast for her name. She was a great servant and was always ready "to do" for others. Then there was Mary who simply sat at the feet of Jesus and took in every word He spoke. It troubled me for so many years that Jesus would chide Martha for serving. That was until I began to understand that it's not one or the other; it's not Mary or Martha. I need to find a balance between serving others and quietly sitting at the feet of Jesus, absorbing every word He has spoken. Being from good Martha stock, I needed no encouragement for serving and helping others. What I did need was encouragement for sitting quietly at Jesus' feet to meditate on His Word and absorb all that I can. Whenever and wherever I meet with Jesus in His written Word, He will always be there to provide what I need.

Three Sources of Grace, Strength, and Courage

Did I say there were "three things" I have learned about fishing that need to happen if I want to catch fish regularly? Once I began to establish a priority for solitude, I discovered "three things" that God would use to guide me and provide whatever I would need. The first is an indispensable necessity for anyone who wants to follow Jesus as one of His disciples. Anyone who believes in Jesus as Savior is then called to follow Jesus as a disciple. Each of us must have the first necessity, and after that, a number of other resources and disciplines can be explored along the way. I will share with you two that have become essential for me. I will share the first resource that is a necessity for each of us in this chapter, and then share in the next chapter the other two resources that are essentials for me.

The first and foremost source of God's guiding is His written Word. God may well continue to speak to people in ways I have never experienced, but I am absolutely sure that the most significant way He speaks is through His written Word. The more time I spend meditating on His written Word, the more He works "healing, teaching, and guiding" me. Dietrich Bonhoeffer speaks very clearly about this practice in *Meditating on The Word*. Bonhoeffer has other more familiar books, but this one seems to be a lost volume. Many of us need to find it, because I don't find others speaking of meditating on the Word the way Bonhoeffer does. I find it necessary in my faith journey to practice the meditation he encourages. He speaks clearly about meditating: "What do I want from my meditation? We want in any case to rise up from our meditation in a different state from when we sat down. We want to meet Christ in his Word. We turn to the text in our desire to hear what it is that he wants to give us and teach us through his Word. His fellowship, his teaching, his guidance for the day through his Word—that is the goal. Thus you will begin the day freshly strengthened in your faith".[18]

Bonhoeffer makes it very clear, "We want to meet Christ in his Word." We are not considering words, or concepts, or thoughts on a page. Bonhoeffer says we want to meet Jesus as He speaks to us and supplies us with all that we need. I have never seen anyone else share it quite so clearly and so profoundly: "We want to meet Christ in his Word." That absolutely defines the time of solitude that we spend meditating on the Word as time spent with Jesus.

Everywhere we go in Scripture we find Jesus. We know that is true in the four gospels that record His teaching, preaching, and acts of power. It would be employing a very narrow definition of inspiration to think that these four books were the only places Jesus speaks. Jesus uses all of the written Word to speak to us and to guide our lives. As we follow Jesus faithfully, He uses all of Scripture for our learning. Even in Genesis Chapter 1, we read clearly of the Father's creative work and the power of His Word as He says, "Let there be. . . " It is also clear in Genesis 1 that "The Spirit of God was hovering over the waters" (Genesis 1:2), so the third person of the Trinity is present. It is not until the Gospel of John makes it clear that we come to understand without a doubt that Jesus was also present since before the creation of the world. John testifies, "In the beginning was the Word, and the Word was with God, and the Word was God. He was with God in the beginning. Through him all things were made; without him nothing was made that has been made" (John 1:1–3).

While Jesus didn't appear bodily until he was born in Bethlehem's manger, He is part of the Triune God. As one of the three persons of the Trinity, He has always been active throughout the history of the world. With the Father and the Spirit, Jesus has been involved in the lives of patriarchs, prophets, and kings. Jesus uses the Word recorded since the Pentateuch to guide the lives of all who seek to follow Him. Even today,

Jesus speaks to us through the rich words of the Psalms and the apostles of the New Testament.

Regardless of the place in Scripture that may be the focus of one's meditation, Bonhoeffer affirms, "We want to meet Christ in his Word." For those of us who live on planet Earth after Jesus walked, and taught, and died and rose, it is Jesus we follow as His disciples. Only because of the amazing grace of the Father, always guided by the leading of the Spirit, do we seek to follow Jesus as surely as the twelve walked right beside Him. From Genesis to Revelation, we seek Jesus to lead, guide, direct, and strengthen us to follow Him every step of every day. Bonhoeffer encourages us to go to a much deeper place than just reading words about Jesus. He encourages us to use the Word to meet daily with Jesus in solitude as we meditate on His written Word. In the written Word is where we discover Jesus and what we need to follow Him.

A Most Unique Practice Found Only in Bonhoeffer

There is one other thing I find in Bonhoeffer that I have never seen anywhere else. It is a unique practice that I have seen no one else emphasize, and it has greatly enriched the time I spend with Jesus in His Word. Here is what Bonhoeffer promotes: "What text and how long should the text be? It has proven helpful to meditate on a text of approximately ten to fifteen verses for a period of a week. It is not good to meditate on a different text each day, since we are not always equally receptive, and the texts for the most part are much too long for that".[19]

The profound wisdom offered here has led me to find myself hanging onto this practice since well before the first trip to the desert of Big Bend. Meditating on the same text for a week is best because I am not always equally receptive. It also helps me go deeper when holding onto the same Words of Jesus for a longer period of time. I can find Jesus in all of Scripture, but John 15:1–11 is one of my favorites. These are clearly Jesus' words for disciples to hold onto, seeking a deeper understanding. Jesus specifically says, "Remain in me, and I will remain in you. No branch can bear fruit by itself; it must remain in the vine. Neither can you bear fruit unless you remain in me" (John 15:4). All of this "remain" language is clearly the focus of this passage. Jesus repeats it twelve times in eleven verses, making a living, growing relationship with Him absolutely essential to our effectiveness in His Kingdom. The other word repeated seven times is "fruitful." Jesus says plainly that without the life-giving connection to Him, we "can do nothing."

If verse 4 were not enough, Jesus repeats almost the same thought in verse 5: "I am the vine; you are the branches. If a man remains in me and I in him, he will bear much fruit; apart from me you can do nothing" (John 15:5). I suspect that as emphatic as Jesus is in this text, I will spend each day until He takes me home seeking to integrate into my faith and life more fully this, "Remain in me and I will remain in you." So much of our life as a disciple is a life-long process of coming to follow Him more faithfully. I also love the way that Eugene Peterson phrases John 15:5 in *The Message*: "I am the Vine, you are the branches. When you are joined with me and I with you, the relationship intimate and organic, the harvest is sure to be abundant." This is why this relationship with Jesus, "intimate and organic," is by God's grace a life-long endeavor.

Chapter Six: Questions for Reflection or Sharing

"Remain in me, and I will remain in you. No branch can bear fruit by itself; it must remain in the vine. Neither can you bear fruit unless you remain in me." (John 15:5)

In the rhythm of your life, is your more creative time for solitude and prayer in the morning at the beginning of your day, or in the evening at the close of your day?

What might encourage you to be intentional to "slow the pace and quiet the noise" in your life and let Jesus renew your spirit?

"Rest, Relax, Renew, Restore, Regenerate:" What do these words feel like as you consider them?

As you spend time quietly meditating on the Word of God, what difference would it make to imagine yourself actually meeting with Jesus?

What would it be like for you to practice Bonhoeffer's encouragement to meditate on the same ten to fifteen verses for a week?

What other ways have you discovered to take Jesus at His word to "remain in me and I will remain in you?"

CHAPTER SEVEN

MORE DEVOTIONAL PATTERNS FOR STAYING CURRENT WITH JESUS

"Let me be wise to draw from every dispensation of Thy providence the lesson Thou art mindful to teach me. Give me a stout heart to bear my own burdens. Give me a willing heart to bear the burdens of others. Give me a believing heart to cast all my burdens on Thee."

—John Baillie

Throughout the history of God's relationship with His people, He has raised up extraordinary models of humble men and women of faith. Many of their struggles in prayers and songs have strengthened God's people throughout the centuries. Many of these prayers and songs are recorded in Scripture, and even more modern expressions of struggles in prayers and songs are available to us today. Praying and singing with these pioneers of faithfulness are good for the soul.

The Other Two Most Significant Patterns for This Follower of Jesus

Whether it's about the corporate worship of any Church Family or the solitude of any follower of Jesus, the written Word of God is the indispensable necessity that provides both direction and strength for anyone who wants to follow Jesus. It seems impossible to follow Jesus apart from His written Word, and following Jesus must be the goal of every disciple. Along the way are a number of other disciplines or patterns that followers of Jesus have practiced. Each in its own way encourages faithfulness in following Jesus, and provides grace, and strength and courage.

While fasting seems practiced by so few as a spiritual discipline today, it can be one of those patterns. While regularly mentioned in Scripture, few followers of Jesus practice it today. Others practice a lifestyle of simplicity as a spiritual discipline in following Jesus. Several denominations are known for practicing a simple lifestyle. For others the spiritual discipline of service encourages faithfulness in discipleship. Those who serve among the poor or physically challenged especially practice their faithfulness in their service.

Two particular devotional patterns or resources that I've discovered are especially helpful to me in following Jesus. In my times of solitude I find prayer in response to meditation on the Word to be very significant. I also find singing the hymns and songs of the Church to be especially strengthening. I am not suggesting these are the two most significant resources, only that I have discovered them to be so for my journey following Jesus. Whenever anyone asks me what helps, I generally encourage an individual to explore those patterns or resources that he or she seems to find interesting. If it seems helpful, then hang onto it and explore its depths in following Jesus.

Only a week ago I accompanied a group on a mission trip to serve in Central America. In the last evening's devotion, the leader asked the question: "Which is more important, to pray prayers written by others, or to pray the prayers that come from your heart?" It was an honest question, as he said he was seeking to grow in this area of his journey of faith. Part of the reason that he had asked the question was because another of the missionaries had a prayer book that had belonged to his grandmother and was over one hundred years old. On the previous evenings he had shared several of those prayers, and they had been helpful to the group.

My answer to the devotion leader's question was an absolute, "*Yes!*" For the last thirty-five years my answer has been, "Both," and I find each helpful for different reasons. If all I do is pray from my own heart and mind, my prayers remain rather personal and parochial and involve only my own small world. If all I do is pray the prayers of others, there are many for whom I am personally concerned that get left out. I need both prayers to enrich and deepen my own prayer life.

John Baillie's *A Diary of Private Prayer*

Since April of 1980, the written prayers that have enriched my prayer time have come from John Baillie's *A Diary of Private Prayer.* Earlier in this chapter, I quoted from his prayer for the morning of worship. It is said of John Baillie that there were three important pieces of furniture that filled his office. First was his desk where he would read, study, and meditate on the Scripture. Second, were the chairs he used to visit with people who sought his wisdom and his encouragement. Third, was the kneeler near the window where he prayed. If you live with his prayers very long, it is easy to sense that they were born from and refined by the hours he spent in prayer. John Baillie and his prayers for each morning and evening of each day of the month continue to encourage and motivate me toward a life of prayer.

Many things about the Baillie prayers are edifying to me. If forced to select just four reasons these prayers are so significant for me, the following would be on my list.

1. I need his regular reminders that this is not home. It is so easy subtly to forget that I am on a journey toward a heavenly home. By faith in Jesus, I, and all who have faith in Him, have a place prepared in the Father's house where we will spend an eternity. Whenever I get caught up in the activities of life and the world, I can forget that this is not home. In his prayer for the morning of the fifteenth day, he reminds me: "Let me remember that here I have not a continuing city, but only a place of sojourn and a time of testing and training".[20] Again in his prayer for the morning of the thirty-first day, he reminds me: "Grant rather that each day may do something so to strengthen my hold upon the unseen world, so to increase my sense of its reality, and so to attach my heart to its holy interests that, as the end of my life draws ever nearer, I may not grow to be a part of these fleeting earthly surroundings, but rather grow more and more conformed to the life of the world to come".[21] I need reminders such as these that this is not home.

2. When all I do is pray my own prayers, I narrow my focus to my own small world. I will continue to pray for the people for whom I have concern and the mission and ministry causes with which I am most familiar. I also need to stay aware of God's larger concerns for His work across the world. He is concerned for me and my family and friends, but He also has a whole world out there about which He is equally concerned. Baillie begins his prayer for the evening of the eighth day like this: "O God, the Father of all mankind, I would bring before Thee to-night

the burden of the world's life. I would join myself to the great scattered company of those who, in every corner of every land, are now crying out to Thee in their need".[22] By the way, Baillie does pray in "Thee's" and "Thou's," but I have lived with his prayers for so long that when I pray them, they automatically become "You" and "Your." John regularly lifts my eyes to see God's view of and concern for His people of the whole world He created. I need someone to expand my sight to seek to look at the world as God does.

3. I love it that Baillie's prayers are thoroughly interwoven with Scripture. Sometimes, it's a phrase here and there that attracts your notice only as you live longer with his writings in *A Diary of Private Prayer*. At other times, a verse of Scripture will be included as part of his prayer. On some days, he leads you to pray selected verses of the Word, and sometimes the whole prayer is nothing but Scripture. On the morning of days eight and eighteen, and the evening of the thirtieth day, he leads the pray-er to reflectively pray the verses he chooses. For instance, on the eighteenth day he leads the prayer: "Jesus Christ said, 'Love your enemies.' O God, incline my heart to follow in this way. Jesus Christ said, 'Watch and pray, that ye enter not into temptation.' O God, incline my heart to follow in this way".[23] It is a powerful pattern to meditate on Jesus' words and then to pray, "O God, incline my heart to follow in this way." On other days he leads the pray-er just to pray the Scripture, with no other words of reflection or meditation. He simply encourages reading, meditating, and praying the Scripture. On the tenth morning and the twentieth evening, the page is filled with nothing but Scripture passages. On the twentieth evening, John leads us to pray Psalm 103:1–5. This has always

been significant for me, because Psalm 103 was my maternal grandmother's favorite Scripture verse. Living with these prayers of John's was the beginning of my learning to explore, and specifically, to pray the Scriptures.

4. As significant as each of these reasons is in my journey of faith, the fourth pattern in Baillie's prayers has to be at the top of my list. I think this is saving the best for last. It took me quite some time even to notice it, but Baillie regularly includes some powerful formation prayers as you walk with him through the month. At times, it is as simple as the second morning when we pray: "Speak Thou in my words today, think in my thought, and work in all my deeds".[24] The morning of the fourth day closes with: "Suggest, direct, control every movement of my mind; for my Lord Christ's sake".[25] In a fuller way, John leads us to pray on the morning of the twenty-first day: "Inspire all my thoughts. Pervade all my imaginations. Suggest all my decisions. Lodge in my will's most inward citadel and order all my doings".[26]

Each of these prayers request in the most fervent manner—Jesus, You take charge in my life and I will follow You wherever You would lead me to go! Perhaps none is more comprehensive of all of life than the third example of a formation prayer from the twenty-first day. To pray "Inspire, Pervade, Suggest, Lodge, and Order" is inclusive of all that I am, and do, and hope to become. I find that the more that I pray these prayers, the more I have to stop and ask myself if I really want to pray like this. I must honestly admit that there have been days or periods when I have not wanted this prayer. To grow and let Jesus mature me in this journey of faith, I need to come back and pray them again and again.

The prayer for the morning of the twenty-sixth day says it so clearly and simply. Baillie leads us to pray: "Let Christ be formed in me...".[27] It's a prayer to pray over and over, and it brings together all the words of all formation prayers clearly and simply, "Let Christ be formed in me...." It is very similar to the Baillie prayer quoted earlier in a previous chapter: "May Jesus Christ be today the companion of my thoughts, so that His Spirit may more and more take root in me," which is exactly what Jesus wants to do in the life of everyone who follows Him!

The Third Source for Grace, Strength, and Courage

Several chapters ago, I shared the story of my week in the desert of Big Bend National Park in January of 1990. It was singing the songs and hymns of the Church that cut the fear of that first night and has been calming for many nights to follow. That was when it became so obvious to me that singing the songs of faith was powerful for good. I actually grew up in a home where singing together was our family practice. This practice seems really strange in today's world, but our mother played the piano and we all gathered around to sing. It was in the desert of Big Bend that I came to the striking realization of just how formative the hymns and songs of the faithful had been to my faith and life. I know many other followers of Jesus for whom the same is true, some, who like me also sing, and others who listen to these songs on an iPod or cell phone.

Singing with a sanctuary or worship center filled with energetic, faithful disciples is good for the soul. In a smaller group of fervent followers of Jesus, in a home or around a fire, singing songs of faith can be deeply meaningful. Even in the hospital room of a critically ill person, singing "Beautiful Savior" with the family can bring inspiring peace, comfort, and strength. Each of these settings for singing can have a profound effect on the singers, but none of these is the setting of which I want to speak.

I am profoundly affected when I sing the songs of our faith alone on a retreat for solitude, or in the morning solitude of my office while watching the sunrise. It touches me deeply to sing these hymns and songs and dwell on the richness of the texts. Sometimes the richness comes from knowing the background or setting in which a text was written. At other times, the words themselves carry the praise, prayer, or adoration that I need to give to our incredible God.

Singing the words of Scripture quietly, meditatively, enables the solitary singer to sense the Spirit of Jesus who is always present. About ten years ago, I was in Tennessee leading a prayer retreat for church workers. I had them focus on Psalm 46:10 where, in this psalm of confident trust in God, suddenly God speaks: "Be still, and know that I am God." A hospital chaplain, who attended, said, "You know that this is also a song, don't you?" I asked him to teach it to us, which he was glad to do. Its simple tune, with a powerful text straight from the mouth of God, enables us to sing the Scriptures.

Praying the Scriptures, as mentioned earlier in this chapter, goes much deeper than my meager words of prayer. It is even more powerful when I can pray the Scripture in song. To sing as many times as I need, "Be still and know that I am God," goes deep inside to calm and quiet and bring the stillness to my spirit that I believe God intends. It is the power of singing in solitude; the quality of the voice is completely irrelevant. My practice of singing alone does much to enable Jesus to bring me the grace, strength, and courage that I need and that He wants to provide.

Often, to sing the name of Jesus or the names by which we know Jesus from the Scripture, can be strengthening. One of the simple songs that is very helpful to me in this regard is "Jesus, Name above All Names." It's almost impossible for me to write this without singing it as I do. The words and the melodies become a part of you. They stick with you throughout the day to be sung or hummed whenever or wherever.

It is a constant reminder of the Jesus who promises, "And surely I will be with you always to the very end of the age" (Matthew 28:20b). It's what happens as you sing the hymns of the faith alone. It's a deep reminder of the presence of Jesus.

In the collection of hymns or songs that I sing regularly in solitude, there have to be some powerful hymns of praise and adoration. One of the hymns in my collection is, "Alleluia! Let Praises Ring!" I love it for several reasons; first is the powerful tune that enables the singer to present this adoration to God with great energy. Second, I love hymns that repeat the almost indefinable word, "alleluia." The best Webster can do to define it is to say that it is "a shout or song of praise or thanksgiving." Third, I love hymns that are so Trinitarian, giving praise and adoration to our God-Father, Son, Spirit! One of my most memorable moments of praise with this hymn goes back to that week in Big Bend when I was led to sing it with great energy as the sun was rising over the Sierra Del Carmen mountains in the east.

Alleluia! Let praises ring! To God the Father let us bring Our songs of adoration.

To him through everlasting days Be worship, honor, pow'r, and praise,

Whose hand sustains creation.

Singing, Ringing: Holy, holy, God is holy; Spread the story

Of our God, the Lord of glory.[28]

Another hymn that I would share, this one far more contemporary and whose author is Herbert Brokering, is simply titled, "Stay with Us." (This hymn can be found in the Lutheran Service Book, #879. Or just

Google it.) It was a gracious act of God to have a very good pastor friend of mine, who knows far more hymns than I do, share this one with me about one month into "my new reality." After he shared it with me, I have no idea how many consecutive mornings I began my morning solitude with "Stay with Us." Neither can I tell you how many times I have gone back to it. It continues to enable Jesus to give me the grace, strength, and courage that I have so needed. It's rather short, kind of simple, yet very profound.

Those who are familiar with Brokering hymn texts know he always seems to get the word "surprise" included. In this hymn text, it is so exactly what I need. I have needed Jesus to surprise me in just the ways that He knew I needed. I am so glad Brokering used the plural pronoun "us," because it has led me to be intentional to pray this so many times for me and for my wife, Vonnie. I also love that the song begins with a word of praise.

This was indeed a great loss for both of us. It felt like thirty-eight years of relationships were ripped from our lives. I prayed in song, over and over, for Jesus to keep us close and provide the grace and strength we needed for these months of loss. The third and fourth verses of this song have been the most significant for me. Moments of grief are very unpredictable. Some you can anticipate, but more often than not they will suddenly pop up when you see a picture, hear someone's voice, or think some random thought and the feelings come rushing back. The sadness, fear, or anger washes over you, and it is most helpful to pause and experience them. It is not pleasant, but this is what grief does.

I have no idea what led Brokering to a phrase about a road that will bend, but nothing could be more descriptive of my experience since January 27, 2014. In sixty-four years of life, the road has never taken a bend like this one. This is how I would pray regularly for Jesus to be with us, as our road has taken a huge bend. I prayed for Jesus to give us strength to deal with our tears and our fears, especially the fears about what in the world happens next. Above all, it was powerfully comforting to pray for Jesus to carry us and this heavy load. This verse did so much to define the loss and pain with which we were dealing and encourage us to know that Jesus was with us every step of every day. It led naturally to verse four, which brought us back to the hope in Jesus that we so much needed.

The next verse so perfectly follows the previous. It leads us from the tears and fears to a joy in life to which Jesus would be leading us. So we continued to pray in song for Jesus to keep us close until He would bring us to the place when we could see for ourselves this new joy in life, as we let go of the old and embraced what He was unfolding before us. I would pray: "In the process, Jesus, we will need You to heal our eyesight in order for us to be able to see the future You are preparing. This is really, really difficult stuff, Jesus. So we need You to heal our vision of what could be."

Right here is the only place I would have loved a chance to talk with Herb about his wording, and the liberty I have taken to sing the prayer a little differently. He closes this verse with a request for Jesus to move us toward the light. For me, I keep hearing Jesus saying, "I am the light of the world," which leads me to sing this part of the prayer for Jesus to be for me the light. I hope he is okay with my small liberty with his incredible hymn.

For a disciple of Jesus who seeks to follow Him every step of every day, eternity is always part of our consciousness. So very appropriately, his last verse points us to Jesus coming in glory...Jesus is coming back! While it's been almost two thousand years since He made the promise, the reality for the faithful remains the same. He is coming back! When He does, everyone will see Him in Glory that none of us have ever seen. Until He comes, we pray for Jesus to keep us strong in faith and to strength us in our faithfulness in following Him.

For the last several years, I have begun my morning solitude by singing a song or hymn. That means not just thinking it through as if I were singing. That means actually singing it aloud, even when I am alone. If I do need to sing something late at night because I can't go to sleep, while I lay in bed with my bride of forty-four years, I then will sing it in my mind as if I were singing it aloud. It's not quite as helpful as singing it aloud, but it's much more conducive to a happy marriage.

I do not know if others are intentional about this sort of devotional singing in solitude, but I continue to find it increasingly strengthening. Luther was the one who said, "He who sings prays twice." The Book of Psalms was the songbook of the Old Testament people of God. It is a good thing that in recent years we have returned to tunes that allow us to sing them again. I am told that singing touches us more deeply because it accesses both sides of the brain. Even if I could not explain it completely, I would continue to sing in solitude, because Jesus continues to use it to enable me to find His grace, and strength, and courage.

Chapter Seven: Questions for Reflection or Sharing

Singing, Ringing: Holy, Holy, God is Holy; Spread the story of our God, the Lord of Glory. (Lutheran Worship, #437)

Do you have a book of prayers that you find helpful, or do you find yourself most often praying from the heart? How might it help you to explore the other?

What other sources of encouragement remind you of God's concern for His larger world of people?

Have you found other spiritual guides that have encouraged you to pray the Scriptures? How have they been helpful?

Have you discovered other resources that literally lead you to sing the Scriptures?

As a disciple of Jesus, do you find singing or listening to the songs and hymns of the faithful more significant? How do either strengthen your faithfulness in following Jesus?

Do you find it more helpful to sing with others, or does it deepen the text for you to sing it alone in solitude? How do you find each helpful in its own way?

CHAPTER EIGHT

RESILIENCE: THE SPIRIT TO RECOVER!

"Not only so, but we also rejoice in our sufferings, because we know that suffering produces perseverance; perseverance, character; character, hope. And hope does not disappoint us, because God has poured out his love into our hearts by the Holy Spirit, whom he has given us." (Romans 5:3–5)

"Resilience: the ability of a body to regain its original size and shape after being compressed, bent, or stretched. An ability to recover from or adjust to change or misfortune."

—*Webster's New Collegiate Dictionary*

Many people seem never to have had a fair chance to do well in life. For some, even the beginning of life was difficult, and life continues to be a struggle. For others who had a difficult beginning, they seem to have discovered a spirit to recover and have even been strengthened by the struggle of their lives. Research into the matter has some powerful things to share to strengthen hope for all.

Rejoicing in Our Sufferings?

I couldn't even begin to say how many years I have been wrestling with the Romans 5 passage. I have actually long believed "that suffering produces perseverance; perseverance, character; character, hope." The part I have struggled with, and the phrase that gets stuck in my throat every time I try to say it is, "Not only so, but we also rejoice in our sufferings." I especially struggle to affirm it when I am in the midst of personal suffering, adversity, or pain. I have always wrestled with where the passage begins, but I have eagerly embraced the place to which it leads, "because God has poured out his love into our hearts by the Holy Spirit." The thought of "rejoicing in our sufferings" is not unique to Paul. As mentioned in an earlier chapter, the book of James later in the New Testament begins similarly with this encouragement: "Consider it pure joy, my brothers, whenever you face trials of many kinds" (James 1:2). For people dealing with adversity, loss and pain, these are especially difficult words to swallow.

I am writing this book to define my personal journey with the "sufferings" and "trials" I have encountered. I write it to share my struggles to be led through the sufferings to perseverance, to character, and to a "hope that does not disappoint because God has poured out his love into our hearts by the Holy Spirit, whom he has given us." Part of Webster's definition affirms that resilience is "an ability to recover from or adjust to change or misfortune." Depending on the extent of the change or misfortune, the resilience required will vary. I certainly do not claim that my change or misfortune is the worst ever experienced. Nevertheless, to have thirty-eight years of faithful ministry suddenly taken from me was the most significant adversity, loss, or pain I have ever encountered.

My Greatest Chaos

This phrase was part of my journal entry for Saturday, March 22. I was seven weeks and three days into "my new reality." I began that morning:

> "Jesus, give me a heart like Yours. Okay, I have to confess that this morning I do not want to pray this prayer! *Wow—* this really sucks! I do not want to pray this prayer, but I will choose to pray—Jesus, give me a heart like Yours and help me to respond as You would. Jesus, I really need You to give me a heart like Yours and a desire to respond as You would. As I told Vonnie earlier, this is the first time I have resisted praying this prayer. I don't want to pray it, but I will. *Jesus Calling* begins today, 'Rejoice and Be Thankful! As you walk with Me through this day, practice trusting and thanking Me all along the way. Trust is the channel through which My Peace flows into you. Thankfulness lifts you up above your circumstances. Practice trusting and thanking Me continually.'[29] And I do have so much to be thankful for. . . even in this the greatest chaos of my life. This chaos has only served to strengthen my dependence on You. It is absolutely true that I have never been so dependent on You, Jesus, and I have never been so carried by You. Now *that* is a thought—The Greatest Chaos of my life! Normally I would say that this is the Worst Chaos of my life! But this chaos has only driven me deeper in relationship with You, Jesus, so it is, in fact, The Greatest Chaos of my life! I want it, I need it, I pray for the grace, and dignity, and strength that only You can provide for these weeks."

Therefore, this circumstance became "My Greatest Chaos" on

March 22 as I journaled. It became the "change or misfortune" that caused me to pray for Jesus to provide the resilience, perseverance, character, and hope that I needed. It had already been placed close to the door of my heart one year earlier. The first quarter's edition in 2013 of *Weavings* was entitled, "Resilience," and it came right on the heels of another "change or misfortune" for the Church Family that I served. Two very gifted pastors from our staff received calls from other churches to serve elsewhere. As other churches began to contact them, I told our leaders, "They are two of the most gifted forty-year-old pastors I know in our national church body."

After the formal "calls" were issued and each accepted, one to go north and the other south, people's perspective on exactly what had happened varied widely. Some approached me and asked directly, "What are you doing to run off these young pastors?" At the other end of the spectrum was a missionary and author, Carl Medearis. Carl had gotten to know our situation when we had hosted him the previous year for a pastors' conference. Carl called me to affirm, "What a great place of blessing and sending to have raised up these gifted guys so God could take them to serve in other parts of His Kingdom." So some viewed their leader as a buffoon, and others as a blessing to the Kingdom of God.

An Ever-Deepening Relationship with Jesus

After we sent each of these pastors and families off with blessing, I viewed that copy of *Weavings* with the theme "Resilience" as a great gift! It was titled "Resilience" and subtitled "Times of Change, Times of Challenge." The picture on the front cover was of a small evergreen tree growing from a crack in the side of a rock cliff with no visible soil. This was exactly what I needed to encourage me to respond rightly in these days of difficulty, and change, and challenge.

I shared in the Introduction to this book: "So, here is the crux of the matter: Regardless of who we are, what we do, where we are in our faith journey following Jesus, whether we are young or older—how do we deal with adversity, loss, and pain? The reality for each of us, if we live and experience very much of life at all, is that we will deal with adversity, loss, and pain! Where do we find the grace, and strength, and courage to endure and to thrive?"

One year before the Board announced to me their "unanimous decision," God had already placed before me the process to discover the "grace, and strength, and courage to endure and thrive." God had already begun to build in me the resilience I would need for these extreme "Times of Change, Times of Challenge" that were coming. Once again, I discovered that "God is always at work doing something before I know about it." That "something" God was doing this time would absolutely provide what I needed for this trial.

In that copy of *Weavings* was an article by Robert Mulholland. God had already used several of his books to shape my mind and heart in a powerful way as I follow Jesus. Two of his books, in the order in which I read them are titled: *Shaped by the Word* and *Invitation to a Journey: A Roadmap for Spiritual Formation*. The second is a resource I continue to share widely.

The title of Mulholland's article in this edition of *Weavings* was, "Resilience: A Rhythm of Life Hid with Christ in God." Early in this article comes Mulholland's definition: "*Resilience* is the ability to respond creatively to stressful, pressure-packed, anxiety-producing situations such as Paul's (2 Corinthians 11:23–29). A resilient person, rather than being deformed, diminished, or even destroyed by such traumatic, tension-filled circumstances, is able to engage those conditions in healthy, redemptive ways that bring some degree of wholeness."

Paul's list of being "imprisoned, beaten with lashes, beaten with rods, stoned, shipwrecked" etc. is more than enough to trump the list of most of our trials and sufferings. Mulholland affirms that a resilient person, by the grace of God, can respond "in healthy, redemptive ways that bring some degree of wholeness." That phrase stuck in my mind and heart for a full year as something that I held onto and that encouraged me to pray that Jesus would enable me to emulate.

A later comment by Mulholland in that same article led me to a more significant prayer focus. He said, "It is making ourselves available to God in the midst of the adversity to be whatever God calls us to be and do whatever God leads us to do to become a means of God's grace in the situation." To "make myself available to God in the midst of the adversity," I began to pray in late January of 2013, "Give me an ever-deepening relationship with You, Jesus, that I might have a creative and redemptive influence on all around me." I had been praying that prayer for a year before the Board made their decision. This was Jesus preparing my mind and heart. I was pretty sure I could not change the outcome; I was led not to fight it, but I could seek to let Jesus use me "in healthy, redemptive ways to bring some degree of wholeness." I knew that if I asked Jesus to draw me closer in an "ever-deepening relationship with Him," He would lead me to be "a creative, redemptive influence."

"Springing Back"—The Capacity for Resilience

The Robert Mulholland article was the most significant for me in the *Weavings* journal focused on Resilience. While the other articles were also helpful, one other article especially caught my attention. Robert Fleming entitled his article "Springing Back" and spoke of over twenty years of work that he and his wife had focused on to bring healing to survivors of abuse. Many had suffered abuse physically, sexually, emotionally, and verbally, but each therapist noted separately that the path to healing for each survivor was very different. Some seemed to remain stuck with problems that became chronic, while others seemed to possess a capacity "to regenerate, bounce back, and even grow emotionally and spiritually from adversity."

The question that each therapist asked about the difference in the healing process and one's ongoing life path was significant. More specifically, what kept some stuck and dealing over and over with the implications of the abuse, and what led others to face it, painfully deal with it, and grow beyond the abuse and the abuser? Fleming responds in this way: "Resilience is the name that researchers have given for this psycho-spiritual capacity. It was once thought that traumatic events in childhood such as abuse, inevitably lead to severe problems in adulthood. More recent research seems to indicate that 'between one-half and two-thirds of children growing up in adverse situations do overcome the odds and turn a life trajectory of risk into one that manifests resilience.' The difference is resilience."

In over thirty-eight years of pastoral ministry, I have always been greatly saddened whenever I have encountered situations of abuse. Whether that abuse was experienced as a child or as an adult, it is always tragic. What Fleming shares is powerful in the face of the reality of such abuse. Tragedy, or abuse, or suffering, or pain need not have a lasting crippling effect. My bias toward a gracious God affirms that each of us has the spiritual-psychological capacity to regenerate or bounce back and even to grow. To add the dimension of growth means we can become stronger, more mature, and better able to handle and deal with the next tragedy or loss that life may bring.

When I reached the ripe young age of sixty-five, if someone had asked me how long I could see myself living, unless Jesus came back sooner, I would have said that I envisioned myself headed toward ninety. That's a good twenty-five years of life and living, and lots of fish yet to catch. I am a hopeful guy, but I am also realistic enough to know that in that period I will have to face other situations of adversity, loss, and pain.

I have no idea what those situations may look like or what they may require of me. I trust that each day the Jesus whom I follow is preparing me and equipping me to respond in a Christ-like manner to whatever may come. I trust that Jesus will provide the resilience I need to face the adversity, to respond with as little or as much pain as may come, and to grow beyond it with the greater strength that He provides. This I believe is how He grows, and matures, and strengthens His followers. It's never easy to deal with loss, but with the resilience Jesus brings, it becomes less of a struggle as I surrender to the direction He provides.

Fleming continues to affirm that "resilience comes naturally to some yet it is potential in all of us, and can be caught, learned, and cultivated by everyone. It is, I believe, a birthright and grace of the human spirit and a soul capacity in all of us to be able to transcend and transform even the darkest moments or the greatest challenges in our lives." Even as I write this, I have to pause a moment and try to soak it all in. This is incredible, great, good news for each of us. Could anything be more hopeful than to discover that the potential is already in each of us to catch, and learn, and grow resilience?

How profoundly gracious of Jesus to begin already to plant this in my mind and heart one year before the January that became my "darkest moment and greatest challenge." The reality is that some of us may need to wrestle more, or with more courage, to cultivate the necessary resilience. Still, the more that we practice this endeavor toward resilience, the more it comes. The more we let Jesus lead us to practice resilience, the more large hurdles become smaller and huge hurdles become doable. My January of 2014 was a huge hurdle, one that I had never come close to encountering previously. It was absolutely one of the "darkest moments and greatest challenges" of my life. By the grace of God and the resilience that Jesus has provided, I will endure this challenge and will move forward to the next leg of the journey of faith Jesus has in mind for me. In the midst of it all, He will have strengthened my trust, courage, faithfulness, and resilience for whatever I may encounter next.

Practice, Practice, Practice!

I have also observed that the more I practice learning and cultivating the resilience Jesus provides, the easier it becomes. It is never easy to deal with great change and great challenge, but it can, by God's grace, become doable. It was not easy for David to walk into the valley to face Goliath, but by God's grace, he could. It was not easy for Jeremiah or Ezekiel to continue to say to stubborn people, "Thus says the Lord," but by God's grace, they did. It was not easy for Paul to face the hatred of the Jews in so many of the towns and cities in which he sought to plant the Church of Jesus, but fueled by the Spirit of Jesus, he did.

In the November 8 devotional, Sarah Young in *Jesus Calling* is reflecting on these encouraging words from Isaiah as God says, "So do not fear, for I am with you; do not be dismayed, for I am your God. I will strengthen you and help you; I will uphold you with my righteous right hand" (Isaiah 41:10). Then she has us listen to Jesus say: "Learn to appreciate difficult days. Be stimulated by the challenges you encounter along your way. As you journey through tough terrain with Me, gain confidence from your knowledge that together we can handle anything".[30] When I first encountered this devotion, I had a tendency to want to skip over the phrases, "difficult days," "the challenges," and "tough terrain." My attention gravitated toward the phrases, "learn to appreciate," "be stimulated by," and "gain confidence from." Finally, I was able to see the two ends of the phrases coming together, and *that* was precisely where the growth was to be found as Jesus led me. That, I learned, was where resilience is found.

Regularly Sarah puts together the two themes of "trust" and "thankfulness" in Jesus' encouragement. In the February 21 devotional, she reflects on Paul's words: "So then, just as you received Christ Jesus as LORD, continue to live in him, rooted and built up in him, strengthened in the faith as you were taught, and overflowing with thanksgiving" (Colossians 2:6–7). She also reflects on the words of the psalmist: "But my eyes are fixed on you, O Sovereign LORD" (Psalm 141:8). Then she has us listen to Jesus say, "Trust and Thankfulness will get you safely through this day. The more you choose to trust Me, the easier it becomes. Thought patterns of trust are etched into your brain".[31]

There is more and more research on the brain of late, especially about the destructive patterns that things like pornography have on the brain. As destructive as such patterns can be for the brain, trust in Jesus can be a powerful pattern for good in the brain of one of His followers. I believe it is true for me that the more I practice trust, the more "patterns of trust are etched into my brain." That practice of trust is one of the things that Jesus uses to cultivate resilience in my soul.

Chapter Eight: Questions for Reflection or Sharing

"Not only so, but we rejoice in our sufferings, because we know that suffering produces perseverance; perseverance, character; and character, hope. And hope does not disappoint us, because God has poured out his love into our hearts by the Holy Spirit, whom he has given us." (Romans 5:3–5)

Have you ever been able to "rejoice in your sufferings," or can you think of someone who has modeled this for you. If so, what did that look like?

Will you look back to some personal adversity, loss, or pain and consider how you might have sought such "rejoicing?"

Who do you know who has found the resilience to engage their pain in "healthy, redemptive ways that bring some degree of wholeness," and what did that look like?

Do you know someone who had a difficult childhood that might have left them mentally and emotionally crippled, yet he or she was able "to regenerate, bounce back, and even grow emotionally and spiritually from the adversity"? How did that happen?

In addressing a personal difficulty, how would it change the situation for you to believe that you have in you "a birthright, and grace of the human spirit and a soul capacity...to be able to transcend and transform even the darkest moment?"

Where do you need to make use of this God-gifted resilience in your life in your current situation?

CHAPTER NINE

BRINGING CLOSURE TO THIRTY-EIGHT+ YEARS OF MINISTRY

"'For I know the plans I have for you,' declares the LORD, 'plans to prosper you and not to harm you, plans to give you hope and a future. Then you will call upon me and come and pray to me, and I will listen to you. You will seek me and find me when you seek me with all your heart. I will be found by you,' declares the LORD." (Jeremiah 29:11–14a)

"Let us fix our eyes on Jesus, the author and perfecter of our faith, who for the joy set before him endured the cross, scorning its shame, and sat down at the right hand of the throne of God. Consider him who endured such opposition from sinful men, so that you will not grow weary and lose heart." (Hebrews 12:2–3)

Everyone it seems wants to "put his or her best foot forward," so he or she can begin a task, a job, or a career well. Regardless of the length of one's career, everyone wants to finish well with integrity and dignity. Along the way and toward the close, it is always important to keep in mind the care, support, and prayers of those who live and walk alongside you. Their significance and importance to a life well-lived is enormous.

The Process Abruptly Brought to Me

I don't know when it happens for everyone, but after I turned sixty years old, I began to wonder about the process of retiring, or at least moving on from senior pastoring. Recently a forty-year-old friend of mine told me of his plans to retire just after fifty, but before fifty-five. He is quite frugal and said he really wanted to get more involved in dental mission work after that. I have another friend who is several years older than I am, and I suspect he will still be going strong in parish ministry at seventy. He continues to bring as much energy and creativity to mission and ministry as he did twenty and thirty years ago.

This may not apply for everyone, but it seems to me that many people move through their late fifties and into sixty with the idea that they need to begin strategizing about how they want this retiring process to happen. Some may want a sudden change, such as, "Today I will work, and tomorrow I will be completely retired; all I will do is fish, and golf, and play with my grandchildren." Others may prefer to have a shift from full-time to part-time, and then phase out altogether in another five to seven years. Others may want to keep at least a foot in the door for an extended time.

Another friend, who works for a large national corporation, informs me that increasingly many people do not get to choose the manner of their retirement. It is decided for them by someone else, or by a corporate buy-out, or a downsizing. So the idea from a former decade that you get to think about and choose for yourself how you might like to make this transition seems outdated. That may be true in the world of business, but it certainly has not become the norm in the world of mission and ministry, where I have lived and served for over thirty-eight years. So for me to think and wonder about what insights might be helpful to a congregation with a history of longer ministry tenures certainly seemed a wise thing in which to invest my energies.

It's obvious that the retirement process was abruptly brought to me. I was familiar with stories of abrupt endings like this, but I couldn't envision the barrage of mental, emotional, relational, financial, and especially spiritual issues that would flood my life as a result. The most pressing seemed to be the issues related to finances and insurance coverage and what my job disappearing meant for them. Having never before thought that my job might be going away, it was a major scramble in those early weeks.

There were far more unanswered questions, but I decided that I would be walking my last five months with my Church Family and then leave by July 1. There were still many of the mental, emotional, relational, and spiritual issues yet to address, but much of that was an ongoing process. It would be a long five months! I would continue to pray every morning, "Jesus, give me a heart like Yours and enable me to respond as You would. Give me the grace, and dignity, and courage, and strength I need to live these days."

Everyone teaches me. Many people in the world teach me what I want never to be seen doing. A smaller number both inside and outside the church, whom I admire and respect, teach me patterns of behavior that I want to emulate. I have known some extraordinary church men and women who, under worse circumstances on both state and national levels, have responded with incredible grace, dignity, strength, and integrity. I have been amazed to watch them and take notes, hoping that if someday I ever found myself in that place that I might have the courage to follow their pattern.

Only As Jesus Supplies the Grace I Need!

Lent came, and then Easter. A very supportive staff person asked at the beginning of Holy Week, "Are you okay? Are you thinking that this is the last time to preach here for Holy Week and Easter?" I told her that I had been thinking those thoughts, but that I was okay. The only thing I could say was, "Only as Jesus supplies the grace I need." Later she asked, "Are you going to have a bad taste in your mouth every time you look back at this Church Family?" I understood why this caring person asked the question. I responded that I didn't think so, but said she would have to catch me in another couple of months and ask me again. I told her that I had been grateful to participate in so many incredible things that God had done in this Church Family and through it for our community and the world. I felt I would always be grateful for those opportunities and nothing could take that away.

After Easter, came the thirty-fourth annual men's retreat at the end of April. The retreat was a nice, intimate gathering of just over two hundred men, of which thirty percent were from outside our congregation. That year, I must confess, it felt a bit like a black cloud of my leaving was hanging over the retreat, but I continued believing, "Only as Jesus supplies the grace I need." That weekend event was quickly followed by confirmation. It was my honor to confirm my granddaughter, along with the rest of that class. Several Sundays later, we attended the confirmation of another granddaughter. Then the end of May arrived, which completed four of my five remaining months.

I remember specifically at the beginning of June having a long talk with Jesus. I told Him how absolutely grateful I was that He had supplied the grace, dignity, strength, and integrity I had prayed for those past four months. I really wanted and needed to finish the same way. I was really sure that all of this was not about me but about Him.

I was really sure that without Him, those past four months would have been a painfully difficult mess. I was enabled to do them, "Only as Jesus supplied the grace I needed." So now, for this my last month of pastoral ministry in this place, I really needed Him to provide an extra measure of His grace!

Three Parting Words of Encouragement for This Church Family

To bring closure to thirty-eight years of pastoral ministry in this congregation, I had three Sundays yet to preach. I would preach the first, second, and last Sundays of June, each with a scriptural theme of my choosing. Three Sundays seem a lot of time until you are seeking to bring together thirty-eight years of ministry experiences. These sermons would be bringing together all of my preaching; eight two-year cycles of teaching Crossways; baptisms; confirmations; weddings; funerals; all the years of retreats for youth, women, men, families, fathers, and children; and many missions trips. That is a lot to bring together in three Sundays, but the way to do so became very clear to me.

The first Sunday in June I am sure it was God who gave me the Festival of Pentecost on which to preach. This gave me the chance I wanted to preach Mission—the Mission on which Jesus sent us when He said, "Go and teach and baptize them!" This message of Jesus has always been close to my heart, whether sharing the love of Jesus locally or sharing it globally in Central America or India. There is a world of people out there, two-thirds of the world's population, who are yet in need of Jesus. The followers of Jesus can never stop going; we can never stop sharing Jesus; and we can never stop loving people into the Kingdom by our words and our actions. On some mission trips there is more action, as with our dental mission, when we go to "care for the least of these" in Central America in a Matthew 25 kind of way. In that case, our words of love for them in Jesus support our actions of love through providing dental procedures for those who could not afford them. On other mission trips, such as with Mission India, the emphasis is on supporting the teaching about Jesus and discipling and baptizing in the name of the Father, and of the Son, and of the Holy Spirit. There are so many locally and globally who still need Jesus.

On the second Sunday in June, I chose another of my favorite texts—this one from Hebrews. I love it because the writer to the Hebrews wonderfully puts Jesus right in front, as he says, "Let us fix our eyes on Jesus." It was probably twenty years ago that a woman asked me after a meeting if I had ever seen a picture of Jesus laughing. I had not, so she brought me one which quickly became my favorite. It obviously helped that this Jesus was standing beside the Sea of Galilee near fishing boats and nets. In my mind's eye, that is the picture of Jesus on which I fix my eyes. I needed to encourage everyone to fix their eyes on Jesus in their favorite picture, or to fix their eyes on the cross, which is the most significant visual connection we have with Jesus. Only one person comes to mind when we look at the cross; hence, the cross is the most significant visual connection we have to Jesus. Each of us can have a different favorite cross image, but each of them will enable us to "fix our eyes on Jesus."

I knew what the last Sunday in June had to have as its text. I have no idea how many times I have put it before this Church Family, but many of them also know it well. As I was about to leave after thirty-eight years of service in Jesus' name, I needed to remind them of God's promise in Jeremiah 29 and the plans He has for hope and a future for these, His people. I was leaving, but *God* was not! He and His plans *were* their hope and future, and He was always faithful. I told them that I would continue to pray that God in His sovereignty had the plan in place that He was already working out for them. Even in leaving, I wanted only good for this Church Family.

I reminded them that the only way to discern God's plan was "to pray and seek Him" with all their hearts. So I pointed them back to Jesus again as He reminded them, "Remain in me and I will remain in you" (John 15:4a). The words and the reality are ever so familiar. "No branch can bear fruit by itself; it must remain in the vine. Neither can you bear fruit unless you remain in me" (John 15:4b). Then I reminded them again, as I had regularly done for several years, "It's *all* about Jesus! It's *only* about Jesus! It's *always* about Jesus!"

It was the last Sunday in June, and with so many traveling on vacations, I had announced that there would only be one Celebration Worship with the Sacrament at 10:30 a.m., after which we would have a Celebration Luncheon in the fellowship hall. Everyone could easily see the crowd in the sanctuary; it was only when we began the distribution of the Sacrament that we saw the people flowing in from the foyer. Well over 1,000 people participated in that worship, and then we fed over 700 of them all the brisket and ribs they could eat. God provided an overwhelming worship and fellowship celebration.

"The View from the Last Pew" or "The One Who Walks Alongside"

This section of the chapter has two different headings, depending on whose suggestion prevails, mine, or my bride, Vonnie's. My bride would title it, "The View from the Last Pew." Even when our daughters were young, Vonnie was never one to sit near the front. She was always about halfway back, near the side. I now believe that said much about her "ministry." Do not ever ask her to chair a board or committee, or teach an adult Bible class, or direct a choir. Do not ask her to stand up in front of a crowd of adults and make a presentation. However, she will lead *anything* with children, especially small children. She taught three-year-olds in the pre-school for fifteen years, and in 2014 she completed twenty-two years of teaching in the Hurst-Euless-Bedford (HEB) school district.

Vonnie is one who prefers to touch people's lives behind the scenes. She has easily done as much pastoral care as I have; hers has always been done in quieter ways, in the back of a class, or in the hallways, or with so many families in our school district. We still regularly run into children, now adults, whom she taught along the way. Often we run into their parents who want to update her on where her former students are now and what they are doing. Most often, there is also given a hug or an expression of appreciation for her influence in their lives. There was rarely a Sunday that Vonnie didn't share some care concerns or visit with people that I never even saw (and I got around a lot and touched base with lots of people every Sunday). I cannot begin to list the legions of people whose lives have been positively touched by my bride in her own quiet, unassuming manner.

To say that this five-month period from February through June was very difficult for Vonnie is almost an understatement. I noticed that she moved from her normal spot about halfway back, to the very back pew. Family and friends would follow her back that way. A smiling, caring face that normally greeted people as they came back after the Sacrament was no longer there. More often, in place of the smiles were quiet tears. This five-month period was very difficult for my Vonnie, as she contemplated leaving so many people she deeply loved.

That's the reason that for me this section should be entitled, "The One Who Walks Alongside." It was not Vonnie's job that was taken; it was mine. Nevertheless, the reality is that a pastor's wife is a *huge* part of his ministry, and that is for me an understatement. She is the most significant human blessing God ever gave me. I cannot imagine life or ministry without her beside me. For all the thirty-eight plus years of ministry, she has always been by my side. Her job was not taken, but she felt that thirty-eight plus years of relationships had been ripped from her life. Like me, her ministry has always been very relational, perhaps even more so than mine. Her investment in this ministry that we shared was huge, and her loss was deep.

Almost twenty years ago, I got a chance to learn what it's like to be "the one who walks alongside." Vonnie was diagnosed with thyroid cancer. I was not the one with cancer, but my life was hugely affected by this diagnosis, because my wife's was. It was not my cancer, so all I could do was "walk alongside" and love, and support, and care for her in every way I could think to do. I so wanted to do more, and I wished I could take the difficulty away, but I just had to ride this wave with cancer. By the grace of God, it has remained a thing of the distant past. That experience taught me to "walk alongside" and pray fervently for God's grace. It also reminded me that for all these years she has been "walking alongside" me, and I have often regretted the times, too many of them, that she has had to go through "stuff" because of my ministry concerns.

I thank God for her daily, and I thank God for the strength of the marriage He has created between us. By the grace of God, we will get over this huge hurdle, and I am sure that God does have a plan and purpose for us. I still wish there was a way for me to go through this without dragging her "alongside"! In the midst of it all, I was very thankful for her job as an English as a Second Language (ESL) teacher in our school district and the love and support she found there. I am also very grateful for how overwhelmingly wonderful our June 29 Sunday was.

One Other Major Note of Gratitude—The Ones Who Pray!

A quotation I have long held onto and shared with many has kept me giving priority in my life to pray for others. It is from Chuck Swindoll in his book, *The Quest for Character*: "There is no more significant involvement in another person's life than prevailing, consistent prayer. It is more helpful than a gift of money, more encouraging than a strong sermon, more effective than a compliment, more reassuring than a physical embrace".[32]

I will never forget a period earlier in my ministry when I was the only pastor on staff while we were calling another pastor and an educator. It was a crazy busy time, and sometimes I wondered how I would make it. I will never forget a greeting card I received from a woman I still consider a close friend. I do not remember the message in the card, but her written message I will never forget. She wrote, "Sometimes I get concerned for you, because I am afraid you are burning the candle at both ends, and I wonder how you will make it. But, then I know how you will make it. You will make it because of the time you spend in prayer, and because of the time we spend for you in prayer."

I don't think that Vonnie and I and our families have ever been so prayed for as in this five-month period. While I have spent lots of time praying with and for others, never have I been so prayed for by people near and far. Being the recipients of this gift is such an incredible place to be. The prevailing, consistent prayer by so many has been so powerful for good. I am sure it is what helped get me and my family through the five months and the time since then. This prayer is what has helped me focus less on the loss and more on the next leg of the journey on which Jesus will take us.

There is one last incredible blessing by way of a blanket. A very long-time friend to Vonnie took her to breakfast the last week in June. The gift of this friend's blanket is really saying something, because her blankets have won "Best of Show." Frankly, that was less significant than the message she delivered with it. She said, "I began this blanket in February, and I didn't even know for whom I might be making it. The more I stitched it together, the more I continued to pray for the two of you, and that's when I knew." The tag attached to one corner of this beautiful blanket reads, "Carefully stitched together with never-ending prayers for Vonnie/Walt Waiser." It made me cry the first time I saw it, as it has many more times since receiving it.

For so many years I have invested much of my life and ministry to this "prevailing consistent prayer" for others. For over fifteen years, I have led prayer retreats for many others in Texas and in numerous other states. I have been given the opportunity to encourage others to the same "prevailing consistent prayer" for others about whom they have concern. Never before have Vonnie and I been on the receiving end of the "prevailing consistent prayers" of so many for so many months. I would never have known that what I have long preached and taught about prayer would now be turned toward us. I would never have invited this crisis of life and career, but I am ever so grateful to be emotionally, mentally, and spiritually carried along by the prayers of so many! *God* is so very, very *good* through His people!

Chapter Nine: Questions for Reflection or Sharing

"Let us fix our eyes on Jesus, the author and perfecter of our faith, who for the joy set before him endured the cross, scorning its shame, and sat down at the right hand of the throne of God. Consider him who endured such opposition from sinful men, so that you will not grow weary and lose heart." (Hebrews 12: 2–3)

In your life experience, how has another person's decision caused a major change for you? Or if you have not had this experience, do you know someone who has such a story, and how has knowing that story been helpful to you?

In your life experience, do you have a story of a major life change that was caused by a medical diagnosis or an accident that was not your fault, and if so, how did you respond?

Have others whom you respect modeled grace, dignity, strength and integrity in the face of loss? If so, how would you want to emulate their behavior?

Have you brought closure to a much-loved mission, ministry, or tradition that had been significant to you for many years? What was that like for you?

In some loss in your life, what has it been like for your spouse or another loved one to "walk alongside you" to deal with the pain?

Who are the people in your life who provide the care and prayer you need for encouragement, and how have they been helpful? With whom do you need to invest more time in care and prayer as you support them through a life change or difficulty?

CHAPTER TEN

THE NEED FOR A DESERT SOLITUDE

"The LORD said, 'Go out and stand on the mountain in the presence of the LORD, for the LORD is about to pass by.' Then a great and powerful wind tore the mountains apart and shattered the rocks before the LORD, but the LORD was not in the wind. After the wind there was an earthquake, but the LORD was not in the earthquake. After the earthquake came a fire, but the LORD was not in the fire. And after the fire came a gentle whisper." (1 Kings 19:11–12)

The transitions in life and the manner in which we move from one life chapter to the next are of crucial importance to a life lived fully for God. The presence or lack of being thoughtful and intentional about these points in life will either enhance or detract from the meaningfulness of the next life chapter. Intentionality about life will always improve the quality of living, and bringing successful closure to a long-held position makes intentionality imperative.

CHAOS TO HOPE TO HEALING

They Never Told Me about 1 Kings 19

My parents were very active in the churches we attended, and that active participation always began with worship and Sunday school attendance. I was very eager to learn about anything that was put before us and almost couldn't wait for the next Sunday to arrive. I remember well learning the story about Elijah and the prophets of Baal. Growing up in Texas, I always looked forward to a good Western showdown, and this was a great showdown on Mount Carmel. Elijah told Ahab: "Meet me on Mount Carmel. And bring the four hundred and fifty prophets of Baal and the four hundred prophets of Asherah, who eat at Jezebel's table" (1 Kings 18:19). Then, in essence, Elijah challenged them to a showdown to prove which god was the true God.

They had two altars prepared, complete with wood and a bull for the sacrifice. Then Elijah told the other army of prophets: "Then you call on the name of your god, and I will call on the name of the LORD. The god who answers by fire—he is God" (1 Kings 18:24). He first challenged the other prophets to give it their best shot. After several hours with nothing at all happening, Elijah began to taunt them. "'Shout louder!' he said. 'Surely he is a god! Perhaps he is deep in thought, or busy, or traveling. Maybe he is sleeping and must be awakened'" (1 Kings 18:27). I remember this story so well, and I loved the drama as the showdown unfolded. I even remember the Sunday school leaflet and the picture of this scene on the front. The prophets of Baal and Asherah kept at it most of the day, but absolutely nothing happened!

Then Elijah built an altar from twelve stones and dug a trench around it. Just to up the ante, Elijah had the people pour water on it three different times. It was Elijah's time to pray: "'Answer me, O LORD, answer me, so these people will know that you, O LORD, are God, and that you are turning their hearts back again.' Then the fire of the

Lord fell and burned up the sacrifice, the wood, the stones and the soil, and also licked up the water in the trench" (1 Kings 18:37–38). This story could not have had a more dramatic ending or a more emphatic statement about who is really the true and powerful God. Elijah got to be the instrument of God through whom God would show His awesome might and power!

I would think that Elijah would have been able to float spiritually for months, after having been part of this incredible scene of God's power on Mount Carmel. However, they never told me about the next chapter. In Chapter 19, Jezebel comes after Elijah and vows to kill him. Instead of responding with a "bring-it-on" attitude, assured that the same God who showed His power on Mount Carmel would protect him against Jezebel, the text says: "Elijah was afraid and ran for his life" (1 Kings 19:3). Now that I was much further along in my life than I was during those Sunday school days, I so wanted to say, *"Really?* How could you, Elijah, turn tail and run after all you had seen God do?" The reality I discovered was that Elijah was as depressed as he would ever become, and he fled all the way to Sinai.

That is where the text cited above comes from, with Elijah needing desperately to be reassured of the presence and power of God. It might seem that after witnessing *fire* coming from heaven to consume the entire altar and sacrifice, the assurance of God's presence and power would be indelibly imprinted on Elijah's mind and heart. This chapter helped me see that God is not always in the powerful wind, or earthquake, or fire. Sometimes it is in the solitude and quiet that God comes with "a gentle whisper." Sometimes I need, or even *desperately* need, the solitude and quiet that enables me to know that God is present to reassure me. Sometimes, if I do not seek the solitude and quiet, then so much noise keeps me from hearing that gentle whisper. I grew up with the Revised Standard Version of the Bible, which translated this text with "a still small voice." This biblical text kept me intrigued about the desert and eventually helped me know that I had to seek the solitude and quiet of the desert. It also helped me know that in this transitional time of my life, which was brought on by crisis, I needed, or maybe *desperately* needed some desert solitude.

Following a Jesus-Led Transition

Since the ninth grade in high school, all I ever thought God wanted me to do was to be a parish pastor. It is precisely what I began to do on October 1, 1975, but as of July 1, 2014, everything was different. I was still a pastor, but no longer in a specific congregation. Several months earlier, I began to consider how to make this "most significant transition in my life" reasonably healthy. So much is written about this transition, and seminars are regularly conducted to lead men and women through it, because it is at the very least a complex, and at the most, a difficult transition in life.

To seek a reasonably healthy transition, I chose to put in place three things that I believed would lead me that way. First, I became more intentional about having a relationship with a pastoral counselor that I knew. I told him that I needed someone with whom to share my thoughts and feelings so that I didn't fall off the road on either side. I stayed in regular contact with Pastor Jim Otte, either face-to-face, by phone, or even once in my boat. He knew the situation that I was leaving, yet could provide the objectivity and expertise that I needed. In early June, I also attended a Grace Place Retreat as a guest of Dr. John Eckrich. Also at this retreat was a psychologist, Dr. David Ludwig, whom I have long greatly respected. I told him, "Either Jesus has me at a relatively healthy place, or I am absolutely delusional!" After spending time with him that week, he told me, "I think that Jesus has you at a reasonably healthy place, but I believe there is yet some grief to come."

I agreed with him.

The second part of my strategy was to begin a relationship with a corporate coach. My pastoral counselor friend had suggested the idea and had even given me a name. I had originally considered my need for a pastoral counselor, or a spiritual director, or a corporate coach. I already had a pastoral counselor, but when the corporate coach idea presented itself, I made the contact. We met in early June for a long lunch just to visit and get to know each other. It was also an opportunity to sense whether this relationship was a good match and one in which we could work together effectively. I should have known upfront that Jesus would lead me to a corporate coach from the business world who was also a deeply spiritual man. Even at the first meeting, as I was sharing a Scripture verse that Jesus was using to lead and form me, this man was quietly saying the words with me. After that, Craig Faubel and I began to meet regularly every six weeks or so.

The third part of my strategy may be a little unique to me, but it is a core part of my rhythm of life in following Jesus. I shared earlier about the week in the desert of Big Bend National Park in January 1990. I had returned about eleven years later, again during the first week in January, to the same remote site in the desert to see if my experience would be the same. I believed I would once more need some "desert solitude with Jesus" in the midst of this major life transition so that I would not get off track. A younger pastor friend of mine said, "I love the way you go off in solitude to seek the heart of God."

In early July, when this next part of my journey officially began, Vonnie and I had a rather rigorous travel schedule. We left in early July for California to help a friend celebrate her sixtieth birthday. After a few days back at home, I left on a dental mission trip to Belize. A few days after I came back, the two of us left for a beach week. We came back home for several days and then left for a long weekend with some good friends to enjoy the wine country near Fredericksburg, Texas. It all seemed even more rigorous as we were living it and traveling it.

I knew that here is where I would need to implement the third part of my strategy in order to stay reasonably healthy. Beginning Friday, August 15, I planned to leave for some time of desert solitude with Jesus. Frankly, even from the first week after learning the news that the Board shared, I began looking inside myself, thinking I would find some anger, anxiety, and deep sadness. About one month after I shared the news of the Board's decision with the Church Family, a man came up before worship and made a curious comment. He told me, "I have been watching you closely, expecting to find anger and sadness, but I don't see it."

I could only respond, "I wake each morning to pray, 'Jesus, give me a heart like Yours and help me to respond in a Christ-like way.'" I also kept intentionally watching for the anger and sadness, but I didn't see it either. I didn't know whether Jesus was guarding me from it during those five months, but I was not naïve enough to think that He must have just completely taken it away. I knew that I needed some desert solitude to slow the pace and quiet the noise so that I could let Jesus do whatever He needed to do in me. I needed my own "Sinai journey" to slow the pace, quiet the noise, and listen for the gentle whisper that would reassure me of God's presence and power. That is why I scheduled at least one week, or as much as two weeks of solitude, if I needed it.

Back to Big Bend? *Not* in August!

I loved that remote site two-and-one-half miles straight off the main road into the desert known as Kbar. I would have loved to go back there, except in August I believe the temperature there must be close to 114 degrees. I have a friend who once searched the Internet for, "What is the coolest place in August in Texas?" Some who know Texas are thinking there is no answer to this question. She told me the answer came back, "Alpine," which is in Big Bend country, but it is high desert. I went twenty miles up the road to Fort Davis, which amazingly is a mile-high city, the city of highest elevation in Texas. It is high desert, but strangely enough, it was pouring down rain the afternoon I arrived. I was able to secure a screen shelter facility and actually needed to cover up with a sheet most nights.

There I was for my "desert solitude time with Jesus," a time when I would intentionally slow the pace and quiet the noise. I have walked down this road of loss many times with others who have had a loved one who was critically ill. The death was imminent and anticipated, but the grief could not really begin until the death happened. My loss was now a reality, and I would be quiet with Jesus to learn what He needed me to experience in my loss and grief.

I began that first morning to reconnect with Jesus in this new place with the well-practiced devotional patterns that have for many years brought me close to Him. I sang several hymns, went to my journal, read that morning from *Jesus Calling*, spent time meditating on the Scriptures, sat with my good friend John Baillie, and then went to my personal prayer list. One good friend for whom I prayed had a husband who had experienced a second stroke in the previous week and seemed near death. After I prayed for them each morning, I would text them a verse from either "Abide with Me" or "For All the Saints." After three or four salutary hours of solitude, I would grab my walking stick and head off for a one-hour-plus walk in the foothills around Fort Davis. Never underestimate the healing effects of a good, long walk—especially in the pristine air of that area.

Okay, Jesus, I Am Ready!

Whenever I go off alone for a personal forty-eight hour retreat or even when I have indulged in the luxury of a week of solitude, there is always a reentry process. I need a little time to get comfortable again being alone with Jesus. When it's just the two of us, it kind of strips everything bare in a Psalm 139 way. I need to let Him know that I understand that He sees me as I really am (which He always has, except now I see Him watching me), and I know that, amazingly, He still graciously loves me. That is amazing grace!

There I was with Jesus on the first day, and the second day, and the third day, and the fourth day. I think it was the close of the fourth day that I said, "Okay, Jesus. I am loving these days with You, and I love this place. And all of it is renewing in every way, and I appreciate all You are doing for me in this time and place. But I thought I was coming out here to begin the grieving stuff in whatever way You needed me to experience it. I thought there might be some raw emotions of whatever sort that I needed to get out, or deal with, or expose in grieving my loss." As they say, sometimes it's important to be careful what you ask for.

It began with a dream the morning of the fifth day. I woke with the dream vividly in mind. The dream was about me and one of the Board members who had "voted unanimously to go in a different direction." In my dream, this Board member was in a very precarious position with monofilament fishing line wrapped around his neck. The more he struggled, the tighter the line around his neck became, and in his fear, he struggled even more. I tried to calm him down and get him to be still. I encouraged him to relax and let me help, and then I pulled from my pocket the small knife, which is always there. I finally said more firmly, "Trust me," and then I raised the pocketknife to cut the line. I woke from the dream with the details clearly in mind. It had not been a particularly distressing dream for me; I was not the one with the line around my neck. In fact, I remember my first conscious thought being, "Jesus, what in the world do You have going on here?" It was that thought that brought a smile to my face. Then I took my journal and recorded the dream and my reflections.

In my time of solitude that followed, I went to Sarah Young's book, *Jesus Calling,* and turned to that day which was August 20. On that day Jesus begins by saying: "I Am a God Who Heals. I heal broken bodies, broken minds, broken hearts, broken lives, and broken relationships. My very presence has immense healing powers. You cannot live close to me without experiencing some degree of healing. However, it is also true that *you have not because you ask not*. You receive the healing that flows naturally from My Presence, whether you seek it or not. But there is more—much more—available to those who ask".[33] Again my thought was, "Jesus, what in the world do You have going on here?" I continued the rest of my rhythm of meditation on the Word and time for prayer. Then I went off on a very long walk.

Early that afternoon, I checked my cell phone for messages. That's when I saw the text that told me that the friend who was near death had in fact died. Jesus had come to take a faithful servant to the place prepared for him in the Father's house. I remember feeling a mix of sadness at his death and joy that his struggle was over and he was now with Jesus. I spent a while praying for his wife, who was a close friend of over thirty-eight years, and for others in the family that I also knew well. It was both a sad and a joyous time for me, as I knew it was for them.

It was later that afternoon that I checked my cell phone again for messages. That was when I saw it! The text informed me that the memorial service would be held on Saturday at 10:00 a.m. in the sanctuary of the Church Family I had served all those years. That text message hit me like a brick flat against my head. The reality was that even if I were home, I could not attend the memorial service of this good friend and be with his family. It was greatly distressing to realize that "the unanimous decision" of that Board had screwed everything up. They had no idea how their decision had complicated so many relationships.

The Grief Begins in Earnest

Even as I read back over what I had journaled that evening at 5:50 p.m., it is very raw and very intense. From the time I saw that text, the feelings continued to grow. Here is some of what I journaled: "Okay, Jesus—so I am very aware of my sadness and anger! So-what-do-I-do-now? This is going to wear me out! What do I do with this, Jesus? Jesus help me—this is a major load of crap! I came out here to see what *You* needed me to do and *this* is *it*?! I sense absolutely *no* grace and dignity and strength in this. So is what I needed to do out here to rage at the darkness and loneliness? *This* is crap! What do I do, Jesus? How do I deal in a real and intentional way with all this anger and sadness?! Come on, Jesus—speak to me! Is it worse now, because I wasn't angry at them earlier? Think I need a walk—I can't sit here any longer!"

Very early in ministry I had a good friend who was an Episcopal priest and counselor to whom I often referred people. At a later point, his wife left him for another woman, and I couldn't imagine his pain. I remember him saying to me that one night he went into his office very late and "vomited out all the emotional stuff he had inside." I felt that was exactly what I needed to be doing that evening! As I walked, there was a Catholic parish about four hundred yards up the road. I hoped that someone would have left the front door open for me to enter, because that was just where I felt I needed to be, but no, it was locked. Fortunately, there was a small prayer garden around the side, and no one else was near.

I do not know of another time when I have felt so agitated inside, when my feelings were so raw and intense. Much like the first night in the desert of Big Bend, I was led back to singing quietly. There was no one nearby, so I began repeatedly to sing "Jesus, Name Above All Names," and then on to "Beautiful Savior," and then to "What a Friend We Have in Jesus." Once again, singing released the energy of the emotionality that I was experiencing. As I quietly sang these songs of Jesus, the grip of the grieving was gradually released. It was singing the hymns and songs of the faithful that led to the release and healing.

Eventually, I walked back to my screen shelter and picked up my journal. I began this entry at 7:25 p.m.: "Is that it? Is that what I needed to go through to begin to get some of this out of my system? That was as intense a time of anger and sadness as I remember ever experiencing. It feels to me, Jesus, that You were setting me up for this all day: first the dream and then the *Jesus Calling,* and then the text message about the memorial service. It seems that You led me to this episode of intense grief and then led me to the singing to teach me how to deal with this intense grief. It does seem like it was an 'episode' of grief. With this episode of grief, You taught me how to deal with the next episodes of the coming months. Thank You, Jesus! Thank You, Jesus!"

I journaled one last time that night at 9:05 p.m. and continued to be attentive to whatever Jesus might want to do in me and to me while on this desert solitude. I had been saying to Jesus, "Whatever You want me to do and wherever You want me to go, I will follow as You lead." The episode of grief had come and gone, and now I understood some of what might continue to happen, as well as the singing that would release the grip of the grief. I slept well that night and woke refreshed the next morning. Just as a "gut check," about mid-morning of that next day, I got a text message from my son-in-law: "Don't know whether you have heard, but the memorial service is Saturday, 10:00 a.m., at our former church." I just held the cell phone and looked at the text message for a bit to check and see whether there were any leftover feelings of grief that I might experience, but nothing came. Jesus had taught me about the grieving I would continue to experience and the songs I needed each time. God is *good*!

I stayed several more days just to be attentive and to discern whether there was anything else Jesus wanted to do in me or to me; but they were normal days of solitude with Jesus. I then decided I needed to end this high desert solitude with worship and the Sacrament. I knew where I needed to worship and the friend from whom I wanted to receive the Sacrament. He was one of those who had been praying fervently for me in the midst of the chaos of the previous months. It was absolutely the way to bring closure to this time of high desert solitude with Jesus. There is nothing quite as healing as the presence of Jesus in the Sacrament, received in the community of faithful followers of Jesus.

Chapter Ten: Questions for Reflection or Sharing

"The LORD said, 'Go out and stand on the mountain in the presence of the LORD, for the LORD is about to pass by.' Then a great and powerful wind tore the mountains apart and shattered the rocks before the LORD, but the LORD was not in the wind. After the wind there was an earthquake, but the LORD was not in the earthquake. After the earthquake there was a fire, but the LORD was not in the fire. And after the fire came a gentle whisper." (1 Kings 19:11–12)

When was a recent time you needed to be assured of God's presence and power, whether after experiencing a spiritual high or following a spiritual difficulty?

There are many transition points in one's spiritual journey. What has been a recent transition for you. How did it go, or how is it going?

What are some of the more helpful intentional steps you have taken or have seen others take during significant transitions of life?

What are some practices that enable you to "slow the pace and quiet the noise?" Is there a place that it is helpful for you to go to do so?

Has there been a significant loss or death that you have had to deal with, and what were the emotions that came early?

In the grief you have experienced, what are some of the intentional steps you have taken to let Jesus calm you, quiet you, and bring you peace?

"DO YOU STILL BELIEVE THAT I HAVE A PLAN AND PURPOSE FOR YOUR LIFE?"

—JUNE 29, 2015

"May the God of hope fill you with all joy and peace as you trust in him, so that you may overflow with hope by the power of the Holy Spirit." (Romans 15:13)

Everyone knows that looking back after one year always provides a perspective that is not possible in the midst of a chapter of huge change. One moves forward by trusting that Jesus always has a plan and purpose and that He is always at work for good. Looking back after one year affirms that Jesus and His plans are always good and strengthens trust that Jesus is absolutely trustworthy!

One Year Does Make a Difference

Today marks exactly one year since I preached and led worship for the last time in the Church Family that I served for over thirty-eight years. Even though one full year has passed, the memory of how wonderfully overwhelming the day was is still fresh in my memory. It was a great day for God as He fed us all with His Word and Sacrament. In the midst of it all, He reminded us all that regardless of what may happen, He is sovereign over all things and all churches and all people. I remember telling this Church Family that I would no longer be around this place, but God was still going to be very active here. I told them that I would continue to pray that God in His sovereignty still had a plan for this Church Family that I could not yet see.

In March 2015, I was in St. Louis to lead a Prayer Retreat at Concordia Seminary for first- and second-year seminary students (and their wives) and deaconesses. I used the opportunity to stay an extra overnight with a niece and her husband, who had also graduated from that seminary. He had recently received a call to serve a congregation in St. Louis after he completed his PhD. In the midst of our visit, we talked about the worship on that last morning on June 29, which they had attended as part of our family.

While they had participated in that worship and had a sense that it wasn't exactly my idea to leave this Church Family, they did not know the rest of the story. Like almost everyone else who hears of the Board's decision to "go in a different direction in the position of senior pastor," they were shocked. As I have done with everyone else this past year, I was quick to let them know this has been a year that has driven me deeper in relationship to Jesus than I have ever been.

They wanted me to know of the conversation they had after they left worship that day. They had had a four-hour road trip in which to talk as they headed off to take their children to a Lutheran summer camp. They said that they had been wonderfully surprised that the service was so hope-filled and Jesus-focused. I hoped they were typical of those who worshipped that day, because that is precisely what I wanted everyone to walk away with from that worship. I very much wanted them to be filled with a Romans 15 kind of hope by the power of the Holy Spirit. I very much wanted them to know that it is "*All* about Jesus! *Only* about Jesus! *Always* about Jesus!" I pray that their feelings *were* typical of those who worshipped that day.

Intentionality with Grief

Everyone gets to deal with adversity, loss, and pain in his or her own way. I have sought to be as intentional as I could in doing my grief work. Intentionality has been my way to seek to stay as healthy as I could in the midst of my experience with injustice. I have sought to balance my own interior work of reflection, and meditating, and journaling along with sharing the story with others who ask out of genuine concern for me and for Vonnie. While I have sought to share the story with those whom I respect and trust, Vonnie got tired of hearing it and talking about it. I have sought to leave room for her to deal with this loss in the ways that she needs to do her grief work.

As I shared earlier, the real grieving could not begin until after June 29, 2014. The nine days of desert solitude near Ft. Davis last August marked my intentional beginning. I could go off alone in solitude, but Jesus would have to do what He knew I needed to enable me to deal with this huge loss. My responsibility was to show up, open up, and invite Jesus to do the healing work He knew that I needed. As always, it was about Jesus who always knows what I need and how to get me there. As He promises in Psalm 23, Jesus was there to "make me lie down in green pastures, lead me beside quiet waters, to restore my soul."

In grief work, there are specific days and times about which I can be intentional, and others that will just sneak up and surprise me. This past January 27 was one of those days that I needed to be intentional in planning. It would mark one year since the Board called me into their meeting to let me know of their decision. It may not be surprising to know that I had planned to rise early and "Go Fishing!" The day of fishing was planned with two friends. One was a very good spiritual friend and prayer partner who had walked with me every step of this journey and who had also left the Church Family I had served. The other was a friend I had fished with a number of times who had stayed with my former Church Family, but with whom I had more recently had little contact. On the appointed day for fishing, my first friend was very sick and could not keep our fishing date.

Throughout this year, in situations like this, I have found myself wondering, "Okay, Jesus, what are You up to in this?" I knew I needed to be on the water, and my second friend was certainly someone I respected and trusted. I figured that Jesus had something in this that I needed to experience, and it would be good. It was a good day with lots of caring and genuine conversation in which I was glad to participate. The only down side was—we did *not* see even one fish!

Vonnie chose to teach that day, and then I had arranged to go out that evening with two other couples. Both were very long-time friends, and it was the women especially who really make Vonnie laugh. We told stories and laughed most of the evening. Good-hearted laughter, the kind you do until your face almost hurts, can be so healthy and salutary for the soul. That evening was all I had hoped and prayed it would be. The care, prayer, and support of good friends are of great value in dealing with loss. It is also true that friends who bring laughter, good-hearted laughter, are also of great value in dealing with loss. This I believe has been especially true for my Vonnie.

There Will Be Surprises!

Regardless of one's intentionality in grief work, there will be those things that cause surprise. I believe that my times of intentional planning have helped prepare me for the surprises. Please know that there is no way around it. There will be surprises! One of them for me was the day I heard that the new senior pastor had been issued a call to my former Church Family. I knew that they would be calling a new senior pastor, and I knew and respected the man they called; I also wanted God to find them a pastoral leader who would be helpful to them. Nevertheless, when Vonnie telephoned to share that reality, it was like a very cold, hard slap in the face.

When Vonnie called, I was headed off on a fishing trip with some friends. (Yes, this story has many connections with fishing, and beaches, and water.) I received the information from Vonnie and processed it a bit. I tried to look inside to check the feelings that might be rising and to ask again, "Okay, Jesus, what are You up to in this?" It has seemed more helpful at each step in this process to include Jesus in all of my reflections and wonderings. When we made a food stop, I found a quiet time to share the news with one of my friends on this fishing trip. He was a close friend who has been with me in all the ups and downs of this journey, so I told him about what I had just heard from Vonnie to see what it might feel like to share it with someone. Then I pretty much put it aside, or at least I thought I had put it aside.

It had been a long day as we traveled to Canada, so we all hit the bed a little after ten o'clock. I went right to sleep but woke up in the night thinking about Vonnie's call. When I wake like this in the night, I make it a point not to look at the clock. I began to talk with Jesus about it in prayer. Then I was led to quietly sing in my mind and heart that Brokering hymn text, Stay With Us.

I kept quietly singing in my mind and heart until I went back to sleep. Then I woke again with the same thoughts, and again I was led to the same verses until I went back to sleep. About the third time that I woke, I remember thinking, "Okay, Jesus, I guess this grief work episode will happen through the watches of the night." I don't know exactly how many times it happened, three or four I think, but I woke the next morning reasonably refreshed and ready for the day. I shared my experience with the same friend, and then I could put it aside. I didn't think of it again until I returned home and shared it with Vonnie.

A Three-Month Sabbatical

Before June 29, 2014, and my last time to preach, three different congregations made contact to ask me to come and help with a vacancy. I knew what a three-month sabbatical felt like, because I had taken two of them over the past thirty-eight plus years. Especially because of the bizarre nature of my leaving and the difficulty of serving the last five months, I decided to tell each of them that I was going to use July through September like a three-month sabbatical. Then I would begin to look at what Jesus wanted me to do in this next leg of my journey.

Along the way, I began the process of discovering, and sorting, and discerning what Jesus wanted me to do. After twenty years of involvement in a dental mission in Central America, there was an opportunity to get more involved in Central American mission work. I had a mentoring relationship with several younger pastors, and several more came and asked if we could meet regularly, either face-to-face or by phone because of the geographic distance that separated us. Pastoral care opportunities continued to arise in ways I could not have imagined. I continued the process of discovering, sorting, and discerning Jesus' direction.

Then in September, I read a book by Peter Scazzero entitled, *Emotionally Healthy Spirituality: Unleash a Revolution in Your Life with*

Christ. Reading this resource was exactly what Jesus knew I needed. Near the middle of the book, Scazzero quotes Psalm 27, which reads, "Wait for the LORD; be strong and take heart and wait for the LORD" (Psalm 27:14). Then he says, "If I were to identify my greatest sins and errors of judgment in the last thirty years of following Christ, they would each go back to a failure to wait on the Lord".[34]

That statement encouraged me *not* to "grab this bull by the horns," and go make something happen. I was now choosing to wait, to be strong and take heart, and to wait for whatever Jesus might want to lead me toward. I continued the process of discovering and sorting through, and discerning and waiting for Jesus to direct. It was the November 7 devotion in *Jesus Calling* that gave me this very unexpected direction: "Collaborate with Me in this effort by being willing to let go of anything I choose to take away." I just kept asking: "Jesus, did You take this Church Family away from me?" That Friday, November 7, is precisely what sent me in the direction of sharing this story.

Two Unexpected Directions

Craig Faubel, my corporate coach, first suggested the idea of writing a book, to which I responded that Central American mission work and encouraging younger pastors and pastoral care are all in my sweet spots of giftedness. Writing a book was way out of my comfort zone and was nowhere on my radar. The experience of that November Friday was what Jesus used to guide me in precisely that direction. It has been a November through June effort which now finds closure on this Monday, June 29.

As God's grace would have it, I am sitting on the deck of a condominium in Pensacola Beach. This is our ninth year to take our five grandchildren for Beach Week; and, yes, we do let their parents come along, but it is really about the five grandkids. To do this Beach Week is one of Vonnie's best ideas ever! All of us absolutely love this week. Yes, there is also a Thursday of this week booked with a fishing guide, so the theme continues.

When we scheduled this particular week last December, I had no consciousness that it would fall over June 29 and mark exactly one year since that fateful Board announcement. Several weeks ago, as I finished the tenth chapter of this book, I became aware of this Monday date. This place, on this Monday, with the whole family together as we were one year ago, seemed exactly the God-chosen time for the book's completion. Even though it was way out of my comfort zone to write this, as I read the nearly completed book last week in preparation for writing this epilogue, it absolutely felt like a very Jesus-led project. So the journey into one very "unexpected direction" reaches completion.

This now leads me back to the other "unexpected direction" of thinking that Jesus did not want me to serve a vacancy. I had just about completed the initial ten chapters when I was contacted by a church just north of our home. They telephoned to invite me to talk with them, saying, "One year ago, we had three pastors; now the third of them has taken a call to serve another congregation and will preach his last Sunday in only a few weeks. Soon, we will have no pastors." I met initially with the head of their Board of Elders and one other elder and subsequently with a group of their lay leaders. At that meeting, we agreed I would serve as their interim pastor until they installed a new senior pastor.

This also seems such a Jesus-led direction because of the connections I would discover I already had with this Church Family. I preached for the first time on the last Wednesday of Lent. Before preaching, I went into the eighth-grade confirmation class to be greeted by three of them, all of whom said, "I know you because you married my parents and baptized me." Later I discovered that I had confirmed two of those parents in the eighth grade and baptized one of the mothers as an adult.

What began when I preached my way through Holy Week then led to the confirmation of twenty-six young people. There have been three baptisms, two memorial services, and the dedication of a pipe organ. All of this happened in only three months. I was not going to get involved in the calling process for the senior pastor until one of the three candidates happened to come to the Dallas/Fort Worth area for a conference and called to ask if I might meet with him. After that, it seemed only natural to visit with the other two candidates. The congregational voters' meeting was yesterday, and a call was issued.

While serving this interim vacancy was not on my radar, I could not be having a better time. Even though I didn't see it coming, I could not have a stronger sense that for now Jesus has me exactly where He wants me. I have led this Church Family to pray repeatedly, "Jesus, if it's okay with you, please make it one of these three on the short list." We will continue to pray, and wait, and be hopeful that whatever happens, Jesus is working out His plans and purposes.

Hope, Joy, and Peace from God

I find myself back where it all began: "May the God of hope fill you with all joy and peace as you trust in Him, so that you may overflow with hope by the power of the Holy Spirit." God is always absolutely faithful to do just as He promises. I am still waiting and watching for the other parts of this adventure to unfold. I told the Church Family I left that I had way too much energy and passion for Jesus that I was sure that He would not leave me sitting on the sidelines. On that pivotal day of November 7, I sensed Jesus asking me, "Do you believe I can take this Church Family away from you and that I still have a plan and purpose for your life?"

While some things have become, and are still becoming, clearer, I am also still waiting, discovering, sorting through, and discerning the next new directions Jesus has in mind. I am still saying to Him,

"Whatever You want me to do and wherever You want me to go, I will follow." For many years, I have affirmed that I want to follow Jesus. After being driven deeper in relationship with Jesus than I have ever been, following Jesus has taken on a far richer meaning.

When people genuinely ask me, "How are you doing?" they also add, "And how is Vonnie?" This spring Vonnie taught her last ESL class and is now retired. Like most teachers, she feels like she is on summer vacation and won't realize she is retired until everyone goes back to school in late August and she does not. This has been a very difficult eighteen months for her, but things are getting better for her also. It's not her way to go on a high-desert solitude, or talk much about this experience, or write about it. She is still encountering her own ways of grieving, and letting go, and establishing new patterns for living.

Vonnie is intentional about investing in new relationships of her choosing to maintain her circle of friends. She has always been good about pulling people together in groups to encourage community for them and for her. She is also discovering the hope, joy, and peace from the God who is always faithful.

One of Vonnie's earliest concerns was financial and how we would "pay the bills," which is how her brain is wired. By the Grace of God, I think Vonnie has been following the principles in Dave Ramsey's *Financial Peace* since before he wrote the book. By the Grace of God, we had paid off the mortgage on our home the November before the January 27 Board meeting. We literally did not owe a nickel to anyone. That reality and the severance package I received as I left freed me to seek Jesus' leading in any way He might want. The interim position that came six months after I left has more than taken care of our needs.

Several friends have read the initial draft of this manuscript and have wondered with me if I still have significant emotions toward the Board. The healing continues, but the intensity of the emotions has lessened considerably. I wrote these chapters, except for the Epilogue, in the six months after leaving. I chose not to rewrite those earlier chapters to keep the authenticity of what I experienced during these initial months after this enormous life change.

We are eagerly anticipating the next leg of this adventure. There are many things for us yet to discover, beaches to explore, and another wedding anniversary to celebrate on December 20. God is always good and faithful, and He brings hope, joy, and peace out of the darkness as we trust in Him.

ENDNOTES

1. Eugene Peterson, *The Contemplative Pastor*, 1989, p. 12.
2. Eugene Peterson, *The Message: The New Testament in Contemporary English*, 1995, p. 330.
3. Webster's New Collegiate Dictionary, Woolf, p. 625.
4. John Baillie, *A Diary of Private Prayer*, 1949, p. 59.
5. Ibid., p.59.
6. Ibid., p. 59.
7. Henri Nouwen, *Making All Things New*, 1981, p. 69.
8. John Doberstein, *Minister's Prayer Book*, 1986, p. ix.
9. Thomas Ken, *All Praise to Thee, My God, This Night*.
10. Paul Gerhardt, *Now Rest Beneath Night's Shadow*.
11. Author unknown, *Alleluia! Let Praises Ring*.
12. Sarah Young, *Jesus Calling*, 2011, p. 134.
13. Ibid., p. 134.
14. Ibid., p. 39.
15. Ibid., p. 360.
16. Georg Neumark, *If You But Trust in God to Guide You*.
17. Baillie, *A Diary of Private Prayer*, 1949, p. 133.
18. Dietrich Bonhoeffer, *Meditating on The Word*, 1986, p. 32.
19. Ibid., p. 34.
20. Baillie, *A Diary of Private Prayer*, 1949, p. 65.
21. Ibid., p.129.
22. Ibid., p.39.

23. Ibid., p. 77.

24. Ibid., p.13.

25. Ibid., p. 21.

26. Ibid., p. 89.

27. Ibid., p.109.

28. Author Unknown, 1698, "Lutheran Worship," #437.

29. Young, *Jesus Calling*, 2011, p. 85.

30. Ibid., p. 327.

31. Ibid., p. 54.

32. Chuck Swindoll, *The Quest for Character*, 1987, p. 132.

33. Young, *Jesus Calling*, 2011, p. 243.

34. Peter Scazzero, *Emotionally Healthy Spirituality: Unleash a Revolution in Your Life with Christ*, 2006, p. 131.